Elvis Costello

The Illustrated Disco/Biography
by Geoff Parkyn

Omnibus Press
London/New York/Sydney/Cologne

© Copyright 1984 Omnibus Press
(A division of Book Sales Limited).
Book designed by Hanover Studios.
Typeset by Capital Setters, London W1.
Printed in England by Anchor Brendon
Ltd, Tiptree, Essex.

ISBN 0.7119.0531.2
UK Order No. OP 43041
Cherry Lane Order No. 67089

All rights reserved. No part of this book
may be reproduced in any form or by an
electronic or mechanical means,
including information storage or retrieval
systems, without permission in writing
from the publisher, except by a reviewer
who may quote brief passages.

Exclusive distributors:

Book Sales Limited
78 Newman Street, London W1P 3LA. UK.

Omnibus Press
GPO Box 3304. Sydney. NSW 2001.
Australia.

Cherry Lane Books
P.O. Box 430,
Port Chester,
NY 10573,
New York, U.S.A.

Thanks to Jake Riviera, Mary Cole, Steve
Nieve, Bruce Thomas, Pete Thomas,
Dave Robinson, Andrew Lauder, Paul
Conroy, Nick Lowe, Stiff Records, Radar
Records, F-Beat Records, IMP Records,
Columbia Records, Chris Charlesworth,
Martin Miller, Judy, and everyone
constructively involved over the years.

Ultimately it is the songs that count,
not the form or context in which they are
released. If one person finds some gems
he hadn't previously heard, this will have
served its purpose.

Elvis – Thank You!

Stand Down Marg
Bells
S Fran.

CONTENTS

A RECORDING HISTORY
PAGE 5

INTRODUCTION
PAGE 17

SINGLES - WORLDWIDE
PAGE 19

ALBUMS - WORLDWIDE
PAGE 37

SOLO EFFORTS
PAGE 47

COMPILATIONS
PAGE 53

PRODUCTION WORK
PAGE 57

COVERS
PAGE 61

COLLABORATIONS
PAGE 65

BOOTLEGS
PAGE 67

TAPES
PAGE 72

FILMS
PAGE 74

BIBLIOGRAPHY
PAGE 76

INDEX
PAGE 78

ELVIS COSTELLO
A RECORDING HISTORY
BY GEOFF PARKYN

Elvis Costello's first single 'Less Than Zero' was released in March 1977 to little initial response from the record-buying public. The strength and freshness of the song should have resulted in a totally opposite reaction, but these were pioneering days for Stiff Records and the single was only their eleventh release. Working against general music industry complacency and inertia that was rife at the time, Stiff had originality and imagination on their side – and the total conviction that Elvis would break through sooner or later.

Everyone involved felt sure this would happen with the next release 'Alison', for who could doubt that this was obvious Top 10 material – but despite enthusiastic reviews and a growing amount of airplay still nothing really happened, much to everybody's astonishment. What 'Alison' certainly did do, however, was to provide an enticing taster for the first Elvis Costello album 'My Aim Is True'.

Along with another single 'Red Shoes', 'Alison' did a lot to boost Elvis' fortunes, sufficient to see the album eventually rise to No. 10 in the charts. The album was recorded on 8-track at Pathway Studios in Highbury, North London, which is used by many a Stiff artiste to this day. Elvis didn't actually have a band at this point, so he recorded the album with the help of a Californian band called Clover, who made a strong contribution to the recording. As part of some clever Stiff marketing ploys you could buy the record in a variety of different coloured sleeves, and the initial batch released enabled one to have a copy of the album sent free to a friend!

Nick Kent in NME said of the album, "Its often savage extremities of subject matter and attitude are framed around a needle-sharp sensibility for strong musical backdrops, whether it was the raging rock swagger of 'Mystery Dance' or the irrepressible riff of 'Miracle Man', straight through to Costello's oh-so-very-deft adoption of various prime mid-60's pop stylisations.

"'Aim' hits you on so many levels that even if you happened to be repelled by the more extreme aspects (and I've met many who find Costello's revenge/guilt fetish persona totally unappealing), you couldn't help but be impressed by some other area of the man's astonishing talents."

And with the album's release in the United States sometime later, Rolling Stone summed it up with: "Truly dangerous rock 'n roll from someone who might have been termed a hard rock singer/songwriter only a year ago. Call it New Wave if you will – it's still a classic."

Elvis on the cover is ironically surrounded by the motto 'Elvis Is King' – a clear reference to 'the other one'. The persona of these songs is painfully aware of 'the other guy'. He is a failure in love, jilted, rejected. Conventional metaphors come vividly and violently to life to attack him.

With the album doing so well a new single followed in October, and 'Watching The Detectives' was Costello's first hit (reaching No. 15 in the charts) and also the first real chart success for Stiff Records. Ironically it was also to be his last release for that label.

Elvis' manager and co-founder of Stiff Records, Jake Riviera, split up his partnership with Dave Robinson at Stiff and took Elvis and Nick Lowe to a new label called Radar Records, formed at the end of 1977 by Andrew Lauder and Martin Davis. At the same time negotiations were being completed for Elvis to sign with Columbia Records in the United States, and prepare for the release of 'My Aim Is True' in that country – which included an extra track in 'Watching The Detectives'.

Elvis Costello / Alison b/w Welcome To The Working Week

32 Alexander Street London W2   BUY 14   Pre-Planned Deletions

Single Out Now

The first release through Radar was a new single '(I Don't Want To Go To) Chelsea', and was also the first release to credit The Attractions on a studio recording. Obviously much was riding on the success of the new single, but despite being an undoubted masterpiece, it fared about as well as 'Watching The Detectives', reaching No. 16.

This was closely followed in March by a second album 'This Year's Model', which surprised many people who thought it impossible for Elvis to top his efforts on 'My Aim Is True'. Nick Kent wrote: "Nothing's really changed, Costello's bitterness and obsessive vitriol is still there. But, like Pete Townshend and Dylan before him, Costello knows that the true essence of rock as potent music is as a vehicle for frustration. There's simply no-one within spitting distance of him. He has his finger on the pulse of this desperate era and his perceptions are so disquieting because all too often they're too damn real to be strenuously ignored. Costello is currently the best. 'This Year's Model' is just too powerful, too dazzling to be ignored or side-stepped."

And in the Melody Maker, Allan Jones wrote; "Elvis Costello's prodigious talent, we can see in retrospect, was only superficially exposed on his first album. Nick Lowe's production is easily his finest hour: a firm but sympathetic treatment of the songs, and embellishments that are carefully considered. It brings Elvis' sneering vocal into dramatic close-up – his voice throughout has tremendous presence – as The Attractions with characteristic razor blade cool slice across the mix."

The addition of The Attractions constituted a great enrichment and tightening of sound. The production of 'This Year's Model' is deeper, richer, and whereas the songs of 'My Aim Is True' were fragmentary, 'This Year's Model' presents a coherent picture of society.

The first 50,000 copies also included a bonus in the form of a free single – Elvis' country song 'Stranger In The House' backed with a frenetic version of The Damned's 'Neat Neat Neat'. The sleeve took creative packaging to new extremes on an international level with four different pictures, each changing three times covering releases in the UK, USA and Scandinavia. Also the UK sleeve started life with the non-aligned sleeve.

But the differences didn't stop there. The Scandinavian pressing had 'Watching The Detectives' added to the first side, and the US release inexplicably had 'Night Rally' replaced with 'Radio Radio', and 'Chelsea' removed completely.

'This Year's Model' reached No. 4, and Elvis really did seem to be that year's model, but a second single in 'Pump It Up' and later 'Radio Radio' in October failed to extend this success to the singles charts, peaking at 24 and 29 respectively. Elvis would have to wait a little longer for that elusive Top 10 hit. Meanwhile Elvis and the band set to work on writing and recording new material.

One of these new songs 'Tiny Steps' turned up as the B-side to 'Radio Radio', and a cover version of the Brinsley Schwartz song '(What's So Funny 'Bout) Peace, Love And Understanding' came out as the B-side to a Nick Lowe single, credited simply to 'Nick Lowe And His Sound'!

Two more new tracks 'Talking In The Dark' and 'Wednesday Week' emerged in the form of a free single given away at some concerts at the end of the year, but it was their next full release that took them to the top of the charts for the first time. 'Oliver's Army', the first single from 'Armed Forces', reached No. 2.

The new album came out in February 1979. 'Armed Forces' was originally to have been titled 'Emotional Fascism', but in the final event this only appeared at the bottom of the inner sleeve. Once again Costello gave more than value for money by adding a free EP 'Live At Hollywood High' to initial copies. The original UK sleeve was cleverly contrived in that it consisted of several flaps that enclosed the record, but ultimately it wasn't really very practical and was later switched to a conventional format. A set of postcards completed the package.

If Elvis and the band were expecting the inevitable music critics' backlash this time round, it didn't really materialise. Elvis had given enough for them to build him up, but he certainly wasn't about to give them anything to knock him down.

In the Melody Maker, Tony Rayns concluded that the album was a sideways step: "Costello has moved away from the put-down-by-numbers approach of his earlier songwriting. Hell, whichever way it's moving, it's more excellent than not. Who else currently makes 12-cut albums without a single duff track?"

And in the NME Charles Shaar Murray wrote, "'Armed Forces' is an album which contains what I suspect to be some of the best rock music we'll hear this year – and it's good to know that Costello feels compassion for the victims as well as terror and rage towards the criminals – but an uneasy feeling lingers

that this album is intended to achieve considerably more than that."

The light, tongue-in-cheek, Sixties-ish sound of earlier albums is replaced by a plush, thick production which does not underscore the songs' ironies, but seems designed to gloss over some possible weaknesses. However, most of the American reviews were unequivocally positive. "He writes short, blunt compositions that don't pretend to be artful, though they are, and don't demand to be taken seriously, even though they're more stunning and substantial than anything rock has produced in a good long while", wrote Janet Maslin in Rolling Stone.

The American release differed in that it had the '(What's So Funny 'Bout) Peace, Love And Understanding' track tacked on the end of the album. 'Two Little Hitlers' came about because Elvis planned a song called 'Little Hitler' and apparently Nick Lowe pinched the title for himself after Elvis mentioned it to him!

'Accidents Will Happen' was the only other track to be pulled off 'Armed Forces' as a single, but despite two bonus tracks on the B-side and the artwork department excelling itself with the 'accidental' inside-out sleeve, its highest chart placing was 28. This was particularly disappointing as it is one of his finest songs from this period. 'Accidents' also turned out to be Elvis and The Attractions' last release through Radar Records.

Despite a high profile with Elvis and Nick Lowe, Radar had conspicuously little success with any of their other artistes, and the company folded towards the end of 1979. Elvis had never been contracted for a set number of albums for Radar, as each was licensed to the company individually through Riviera Global Record Productions.

Consequently, and not in the least bit surprisingly, Jake Riviera felt he had every right to take Elvis to any other label he wished, and in the meanwhile to release a one-off single through Two-Tone Records (Elvis had produced The Specials' first album) whilst other negotiations were carrying on.

WEA Records, however, had shouldered a mounting financial interest in Radar, and had no wish to see Elvis go elsewhere. A court injunction was taken out to prevent the release of the Two-Tone single (I Can't Stand Up For Falling Down), and for a while it looked as though everything would be in limbo for months.

Luckily a compromise was quickly worked out which enabled the releases to go ahead without delay. Elvis would have his records put out by F-Beat Records, a new company, but they would be licensed to WEA. Thus effectively he was signed to WEA for the next four albums and their related singles.

Following this new deal, 'I Can't Stand Up For Falling Down' was out within weeks in its original form but on F-Beat. Copies of the Two-Tone pressing were later given away to fans at a concert at the London Rainbow. Despite the problems, Elvis started 1980 in fine form, and the delays didn't hurt sales for the single as it became one of his bigger chart successes, reaching No. 4.

A couple of months later a new album 'Get Happy!!' followed, and this was Elvis' Stax tribute right down to the carefully refined Sixties sleeve. The UK sleeves were lovingly 'pre-aged', worn away on the outer sleeve where the raised rim of the label would be. With a collection of twenty tracks, this was a veritable feast of new Costello material. Packed with so many ideas and none of them overstated, this album could almost be the equivalent of a double album from anyone else.

Despite a strangely cool response from some quarters, some of the reviews recognised this and Chris Brazier in Melody Maker commented: "Twenty-track avalanches are difficult to absorb – tracks that first seemed weak have now come up smiling, and others may follow. There are certainly better things for an artist of Elvis Costello's ability to be doing than looking back, but 'Get Happy!!' will do fine for the moment.

"Elvis certainly retains his fondness for playing with puns and manipulating common phrases, which helps to give him his acute sense of the sound of a line, though its overall effect can be brittle, making you wonder if he really cares as much about the substance as the style."

The album was a change in direction, and also a change in attack, with the underlying suggestions becoming more subtle. It was also a strong reply to the hinted, but not fully realised, disenchantment with 'Armed Forces'. This was best explained by Dave McCulloch in Sounds: "It lifts Elvis beyond the state of stagnant-perfectionism wherein he appeared to be lodged with the lifeless, unfairly acclaimed 'Armed Forces' which saw the Elv head too close to perfect, computerised self-parody for comfort, and it would have been too precipitous, considering the seemingly unshakable coldness of 'Armed Forces', to have perhaps anticipated on the next album even further adventurings into those grey, unfriendly areas where Costello's

NOT ON HERE.

NOT ON HERE.

NOT ON HERE.

NOT ON HERE.

ON HERE.

Girls Talk. (I Don't Want To Go To) Chelsea.
Clean Money. Radio Sweetheart.
Talking In The Dark.
Black And White World (Version 2).
Big Tears. Just A Memory. Night Rally.
Stranger In The House.
Clowntime Is Over (Version 2).
Getting Mighty Crowded. Hoover Factory.
Tiny Steps. Dr. Luther's Assistant.
Sunday's Best. Crawling To The U.S.A.
Wednesday Week. My Funny Valentine.
And one more!

**Elvis Costello "Taking Liberties."
Clearing the decks, on Columbia
Records and Tapes.**

Produced by Elvis Costello and Nick Lowe.   "Columbia" is a trademark of CBS Inc. © 1980 CBS Inc.   Give the gift of music.
The corporation logo is flashing on and off in the sky.

considerable talents concentrated on hiding and being clever for no other apparent purpose than hiding and being oh so clever."

There were nonetheless definite intimations that Elvis Costello was treading water with this release. Record Mirror's writer Mike Nicholls connected the obvious influences. "Old soul will never let you down and on at least five of the tracks we have The Attractions playing at being Booker T And The MG's. To some extent this is a shame. Elvis has more to offer than Sixties pastiche and one wonders at a song like 'Temptation', which numbers 'Time Is Tight' almost note for note."

In the United States the album's reception was more mixed, and Rolling Stone concluded that "In a sense, 'Get Happy!!' fails because Costello fails: he doesn't break through. It's a tribute to the force of Elvis Costello's temperament that we experience both his quest and his failure as our own. He's succeeded in making his obsessions belong to us. For better or worse, we'll all ride them out together to the end."

Somehow the commercial success of the album did not carry through to either of the subsequent singles taken from it – 'High Fidelity' and 'New Amsterdam' – as neither reached higher than the thirties. This was especially surprising with the latter as there was a concerted promotional effort with the track available in three different forms – a two-track budget-priced single, the EP and a picture disc.

At the same time as the release of 'New Amsterdam' plans were announced for The Attractions to release a single, and later an album, of their own without Costello, heralding many split rumours that had no substance at all. Obviously someone who writes songs so prolifically and of such a consistently high standard as Elvis would need a whole album each time for full expression. In the meanwhile The Attractions had amassed a large number of their own songs that would not see a release other than on solo projects. The album 'Mad About The Wrong Boy' was an independent and cohesive work but somehow failed to sell particularly well. Taking into account the inevitable comparison to their albums with Costello, it wasn't particularly well received, and unfairly so. Since then Steve Nieve has released a solo keyboards album, and future releases from The Attractions are quite possible.

Costello has never back-tracked by releasing a compilation of material, either a greatest hits collection or live album, but what did follow later in 1980 was a collection of songs that had become obscure or deleted – early B-sides, one-offs, tracks from give-away singles, etc. Inevitably, through the variations of tracks on the earlier albums, this collection differed in its UK and US release. Actual track listings are detailed in the body of this discography, but while being close in terms of track choice, this was a Costello album that had two different titles. The US version was 'Taking Liberties', whereas in the UK this was 'Ten Bloody Marys And Ten How's Your Fathers'. Both titles were carefully chosen to suggest clearly to the uninformed that this should not be taken as a new release in the accepted sense – and the UK version stressed this further as it was originally a cassette-only release – albeit in a deluxe 'gold'-plated cassette and case. 'Ten Bloody Marys...' finally reached vinyl in April 1984 when the F-Beat link with WEA expired.

Under the title 'Elvis Costello Holds A Rummage Sale', Rolling Stone said, "The range of material on the album as a whole makes 'Taking Liberties' seem less like a songwriter's showcase (though it certainly proves that Costello is prolific) than a panorama of production experiments and disparate styles. Two early cuts, 'Radio Sweetheart' and 'Stranger In The House', are more interesting as examples of the artiste's attempts to master country music than they are as compositions.

"'Taking Liberties' most oddly satisfying tracks are those that can't possibly be passed off as anything but let's-fuck-around-in-the-studio memorabilia, recorded with only an engineer behind the board and Costello playing most of the instruments himself. Isn't it lucky we let him get away with so much?"

The album was by nature quite diverse, but simply served to strengthen the belief that Elvis is one of the best songwriters of our age. This was a collection of tracks that had somehow never found their way onto full album releases, but very few writers could hope to achieve as much with an album of newly recorded tracks. Most Costello collectors will have all the songs somewhere in their collections, but to have them all picked out and included on one album is a definite treat.

December of 1980 saw a new single from the band, taking a new track from the forthcoming album as the A-side ('Clubland'), backed up with two tracks from the 'Taking Liberties/Ten Bloody Marys...' compilation – 'Clean Money' and 'Hoover Factory'. The highest position this reached was 60, and was also the start of a period when Elvis and

A RECORDING HISTORY

The Attractions' singles failed to make any significant headway in the charts for quite a while.

'Trust' came early in 1981, and for some the title of the album was quite ironic. In Rolling Stone Ken Tucker wrote: "It's not going too far to say that Elvis Costello's career depends on our misunderstanding him. Impatient and agonised, his image flickers: good guy, then bad guy, then good guy. It's impossible to get a fix on him, easy to be confused by what he says and does. The distance he maintains from his fans, his deadpan demeanour, the clever opacity of his lyrics, the jittery but artful leaps of musical style – all of these combine to form the persona of a man you can't trust."

But even this was a qualified comment, for he continued: "For some of us, of course, that's a damned good recommendation, since the motives and moods of many of today's rock superstars are often too obvious to merit more than passing interest. By contrast, Costello is a model of ambiguity: he's discretion's craftsman."

Melody Maker saw the album as another fine achievement, especially in terms of the song-writing, with Allan Jones writing: "The simple truth is that Costello does have a lot to say, and his talent is articulate enough to express every fleeting emotion, image or thought that attracts his attention, to turn them into songs that are often uncommonly memorable. Elvis keeps his lip clipped, commits his energies to songwriting and gets away with murder.

"A professional songwriter, heir to a tradition broader than most rock 'n roll writers can accommodate, Costello writes well about virtually anything. His songs are rarely as confessional as they appear. Hence the versatility of his writing, the variety of musical settings and styles he deploys. He's an investigative songwriter, probably the best in rock. He owes allegiance only to his own vocation as a songwriter: that's maybe another reason he worries some people. You have to advance towards his songs; they know where they stand, and they stay there. They're meant to sting you into reacting. It's this quality that convinces you that there's a *real* voice on the end of the line; someone who's put some real thought into the grooves; someone who treats his songs as a dialogue."

Some reviews claimed that 'Trust' saw Costello in a rut, but for the most part the longed-for savaging on the part of the critics was again avoided. Mike Gardiner even drew attention to this in his review in Record Mirror: "The law of averages states quite clearly that anybody who produces no less than six albums (including 'Taking Liberties') in four years must be due for the critical pillory and a good time will be had by all. But Costello has managed to produce albums that have each shown a marked improvement on the previous set while always delivering songs that are far more than reheated past offerings.

"As usual, the first impression is of disappointment as he fails to capitalise on the areas he opened up on the last set and then you realise he's taken another worthwhile tangent and you discover even more than you had previously hoped. The Costello formula should be getting boring by now but while he still invests energy and care into his work and then sidesteps the pitfalls with agility and intelligence then he's going to put off the execution a few times more."

For his next project Elvis went for a complete change and recorded an album of country music which didn't include any of his own compositions. Country had obviously always been close to Elvis' heart as some early recordings, notably 'Stranger In The House' showed, but to record a whole album's worth for a new release was certainly a brave move.

Whether the intention was to record a tribute to some of his favourite artistes and songs, or to take a break from writing an album of new material, or both, is unclear, but 'Almost Blue' turned out remarkably successfully. Elvis and the band travelled to Nashville to get the authentic sound with noted country music producer Billy Sherrill.

In the UK the single 'Good Year For The Roses' reached No. 6 in the charts, giving Elvis one of his biggest hits and also a remarkable achievement with a country song – it certainly helped to bring country sounds to a far wider range of people. The reviews of 'Almost Blue' were generally favourable, commending Elvis on the venture. In Hot Press, Niall Stokes wrote: "'Almost Blue' lays complexity aside like a liability and goes for the emotional jugular. The validity of the enterprise comes to rest finally on the quality of the songs, the strength of Elvis' interpretations and the resonances of the arrangements. On all three counts 'Almost Blue' emerges triumphant. With this album, Elvis Costello has broken ranks with fashion and thrown new light on the enduring strengths of one of the most abused of contemporary idioms. Country music – at its best."

Allan Jones said that Elvis had rediscovered the soul of country music:

A RECORDING HISTORY

almost BLUE
ELVIS COSTELLO and the ATTRACTIONS
ALBUM OUT NOW

See them on TV.
Play them in your home.
Now selling more than ever.

XXLP13

"An undoubted artistic success, 'Almost Blue' is both the realisation of a personal ambition and a serious attempt to dispel the prejudice that surrounds country music. Costello forces a reassessment of the dismissals of country as sentimental, bland, cloying. He reminds us that the best country music has always been independent, literate, emotionally valid."

Two further singles followed 'Good Year For The Roses' into the charts – 'Sweet Dreams' and 'I'm Your Toy' – but without the same level of success. In the United States reaction to the album was somewhat muted with many doubts as to whether someone from across the Atlantic could really get to the heart of country. In fact, there were even rumours that Columbia was playing down the album's release through worry that it might hurt his career!

Rolling Stone was sceptical, but eventually gave the album the thumbs up: "What is surprising about 'Almost Blue' is that the star and his group The Attractions don't make complete fools of themselves. Country music isn't easy to sing, and some of the numbers that Costello has attempted are especially difficult. Costello doesn't succeed with all his choices, yet in at least three tunes he does very fine work.

"I'm sure that Costello isn't going to abandon rock 'n' roll for the Grand Ole Opry, but his performance on 'Almost Blue' is no joke, and The Attractions do a decent job as a country band. There is, by the way, a special bonus: 'Almost Blue' is the first Costello album on which the listener can understand all the words."

Apart from the obvious choice of country producer Billy Sherrill for 'Almost Blue', all Elvis' albums up to this point had been produced by Nick Lowe, but for the next album Elvis and the band broke with tradition and worked with Geoff Emerick, who gave the music a much fuller, more rounded sound.

For some inexplicable reason neither 'You Little Fool' nor the superb 'Man Out Of Time' had any success chartwise, but the 'Imperial Bedroom' album reached No. 6 in spite of some very mixed reviews.

Adam Sweeting in Melody Maker said: "If you like the man, there's plenty here to get stuck into. But I'm disappointed that he's been content to polish up manifestos already issued, straighten the pictures on the wall instead of redecorating. Frankly Elvis, I expected more."

The review in 'The Face' made some important points in relation to Elvis' previous work: "The verbal gymnastics are as manic and evocative as ever and for the first time the lyrics are pumped out like a lunatic telegram all across the inside sleeve. But the difference now lies in Costello's position to the music.

"Instead of standing at the centre of a song and firing in every direction, he's stepped sideways and become part of the arrangement. Geoff Emerick's production has introduced irony and distance which allows for fury, ambiguity, laughs and smart window dressing. The balance is brilliant and lets Costello get away with blue murder."

After the relative failure of the last couple of singles, the next two – which were both one-off non-album songs – did fare a little better. 'From Head To Toe' was released to coincide with a tour, and caused something of a stir when it was discovered that WEA were giving away free copies of the 'Get Happy!!' album through chart return shops! 'Party Party' followed, and was the title track for a film – it's also amongst Elvis' least favoured of his compositions.

In May 1983, despite being between recording contracts, Elvis' career took a much needed boost in terms of singles chart success with 'Pills And Soap' released under the name of The Imposter – a name that differentiated 'solo' recordings from group material.

Once a new contract was finalised for F-Beat through RCA Records, 'Everyday I Write The Book' followed with a respectable chart placing and served to stir up interest in the new album 'Punch The Clock' – this time produced by the Clive Langer/Alan Winstanley team who had had so much success with their work with Madness.

"'Punch The Clock' stands revealed as Costello's hardest-hitting collection of songs in a while, probably since 'Get Happy!!'. This isn't just because 'Clock' picks up where 'Get Happy!!' left off with its brassy R&B undertones and assured melodic concision. More, it's to do with this new LP's winning marriage of playful musical imagination rigorously harnessed to a batch of lyrics which find Costello's ability to blow a hole through the heart of the matter at 30 paces burning at maximum intensity" – this was just one of the enthusiastic comments on the new set of songs.

Elvis and the band had once more delivered the goods, as he has continued to do this year with the release of 'Peace In Our Time' – once more under the guise of The Imposter – completing the trilogy with 'Shipbuilding' and 'Pills And Soap'.

'Peace In Our Time' also prefaces the release of another new album, so shortly a whole new chapter from Elvis Costello and The Attractions will be revealed.

A RECORDING HISTORY

15

Every effort has been made to ensure that this discography is as complete as possible, but it is inevitable that there will be some omissions somewhere, especially when dealing with the more remote markets of the world. Elvis Costello and The Attractions' singles and albums have been listed in separate sections with their international variations. Owing to the difficulty in ascertaining the exact day of release, which can frequently differ from published information, listings for the most part include only month and year.

The Singles section covers Elvis Costello and The Attractions' single and E.P. releases around the world, all of which are 7" unless otherwise noted. Country codes used are UK for United Kingdom, US for United States, EUR for Europe, JAP for Japan, GER for Germany, HOL for Holland. France, Italy, Spain, Australia and Canada are detailed in full. Choice of single releases has frequently tended to differ for each territory – and where the choice has been the same, the release dates have often varied quite widely. All singles are credited to 'Elvis Costello and The Attractions', apart from the releases from the Stiff period credited to 'Elvis Costello' (apart from the live B-side to 'Watching The Detectives' – Elvis Costello and The Attractions) and the two Imposter singles.

The Elvis Costello and The Attractions' album section covers all studio releases. 'My Aim Is True' is credited only to Elvis Costello, all subsequent album releases to Elvis Costello and The Attractions. The first three albums have all appeared with different track listings in some parts of the world. 'Ten Bloody Marys And Ten How's Your Fathers' was originally a cassette-only release in the UK (on F-Beat), and has only now been issued on album on IMP.

Unofficial record and tape releases are included for the sake of completeness. The author and publishers stress that these are strictly illegal releases, and have no knowledge as to how these can be obtained. All errors in song titles, etc., are the fault of the bootleggers. Song credits can be taken as for the official releases.

The solo sections cover releases that Steve Nieve, Bruce Thomas and Pete Thomas were involved in before they came together as The Attractions, The Attractions own recordings, and the various solo projects they have undertaken since they've been in the band.

The production section covers albums and singles that Elvis has produced for other artistes – for the most part all friends of his. The covers section lists recordings of Elvis' songs by other artistes – not all of which have met with his approval. In some ways it's surprising there aren't many more covers of Elvis songs, but then maybe people doubt they can do anything to improve upon the original!

An extra section has been included as an index to song titles, partly because the album track listings varied from country to country over the first few releases, and also to enable one to trace exactly where the different versions of each song are available. All official releases are included.

Any additions or amendments will be much appreciated, and can be sent care of the publisher. This is simply a start at documenting the recording history of Elvis Costello and The Attractions, for one thing is certain – Elvis will continue to be writing and recording fine songs and albums for many years to come.

WORLDWIDE

SINGLES

**1. LESS THAN ZERO (Costello)/
RADIO SWEETHEART (Costello)**
UK Stiff BUY 11.
Released March 1977.
Produced by Nick Lowe.
  A-side different to album version.
Matrix note 'Elvis Is King' and 'Elvis Is King On This Side Too'.

2. ALISON (Costello)/WELCOME TO THE WORKING WEEK (Costello)
UK Stiff BUY 14.
Released May 1977.
Produced by Nick Lowe.
  Matrix note 'Elvis joins the FBI' and 'Elvis Is King'.

5. ALISON (Costello) Stereo/ ALISON (Costello) Mono
US Columbia 3-10641.
Released 1977.
Produced by Nick Lowe.
  Promo copy, different mix to UK version.

6. ALISON (Costello)/MIRACLE MAN (Costello)
US Columbia 3-10641.
Released 1977.
Produced by Nick Lowe.
  A-side is different mix to UK version.

3. RED SHOES (Costello)/MYSTERY DANCE (Costello)
UK Stiff BUY 15.
Released July 1977.
Produced by Nick Lowe.
  Matrix note 'Help us hype the Elvis' and 'Larger than life and more fun than people'. No UK picture sleeve.

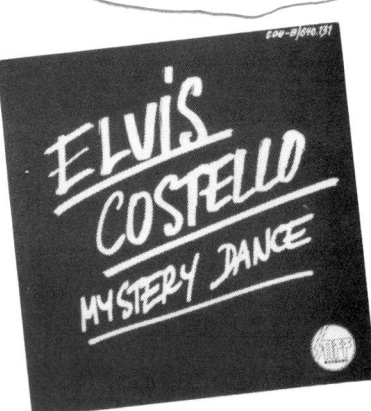

7. MYSTERY DANCE (Costello)/ PAY IT BACK (Costello)
FRANCE Stiff COU-B/640.131.
Released 1977.
Produced by Nick Lowe.
  Yellow vinyl.

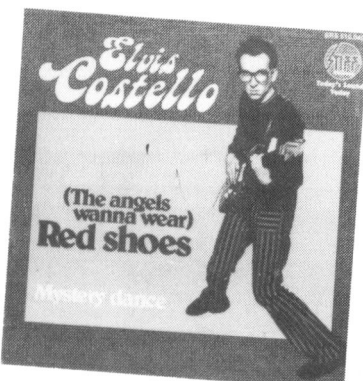

4. (THE ANGELS WANNA WEAR) RED SHOES (Costello)/MYSTERY DANCE (Costello)
FRANCE Stiff SRS 510.040.
Released 1977.
Produced by Nick Lowe.

8. WATCHING THE DETECTIVES (Costello)/BLAME IT ON CAIN (Costello) Live/MYSTERY DANCE (Costello) Live
UK Stiff BUY 20.
FRANCE Stiff SRS 510.042.
Released October 1977.
Produced by Nick Lowe.
  B-side recorded live in London, first credit to 'Elvis Costello and The Attractions'.
  Highest UK chart placing: 15.

9. WATCHING THE DETECTIVES (Costello) Long and short versions/ BLAME IT ON CAIN (Costello) Live/MYSTERY DANCE (Costello) Live
UK Stiff BUY 20DJ.
Released October 1977.
Produced by Nick Lowe.
  Promo copy, B-side recorded live in London but both tracks are different takes to standard release.

10. WATCHING THE DETECTIVES (Costello)/BLAME IT ON CAIN (Costello) Live/MYSTERY DANCE (Costello) Live
US Columbia 1-10696.
Released 1977.
Produced by Nick Lowe.

11. WATCHING THE DETECTIVES (Costello)/ALISON (Costello)
US Columbia 3-10705.
Released 1977.
Produced by Nick Lowe.
  B-side is different version to the album, and same as US single release.

12. (I DON'T WANT TO GO TO) CHELSEA (Costello)/YOU BELONG TO ME (Costello)
UK Radar ADA 3.
Released March 1978.
Produced by Nick Lowe.
  Highest UK chart placing: 16.

13. (I DON'T WANT TO GO TO) CHELSEA (Costello)/TINY STEPS (Costello)/NIGHT RALLY (Costello)
CANADA Columbia C4-8292.
Released 1978.
Produced by Nick Lowe.

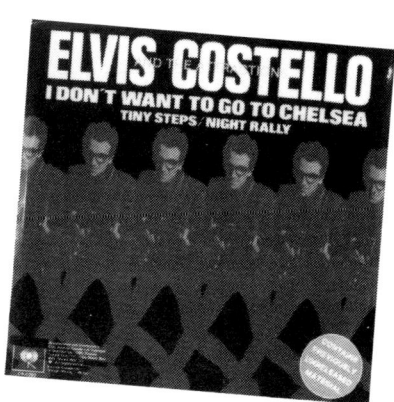

SINGLES

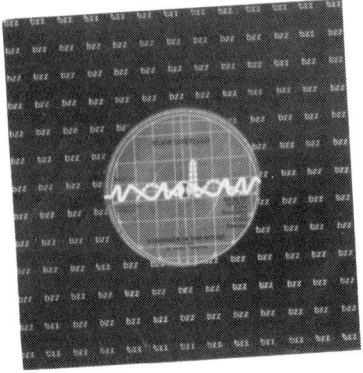

14. STRANGER IN THE HOUSE (Costello)/NEAT, NEAT, NEAT (James)
UK Radar SAM 83.
Released March 1978.
    Issued free with first 50,000 copies of UK album 'This Year's Model'. A-side Elvis Costello, B-side Elvis Costello and The Attractions.

16. NOW YOU SEE THEM LIVE – Elvis Costello/Nick Lowe/Mink De Ville
US Columbia AS 443.
Released 1978.
    12" three track promo single on orange vinyl to promote first US tour. Includes 'Radio Radio' from Elvis Costello. Tracks are not live.

15. PUMP IT UP (Costello)/BIG TEARS (Costello)
UK Radar ADA 10.
Released June 1978.
Produced by Nick Lowe.
    B-side includes Mick Jones of The Clash.
    Highest UK Chart placing: 24.

17. THIS YEAR'S GIRL (Costello)/ BIG TEARS (Costello)
US Columbia 3-10762.
Released 1978.
Produced by Nick Lowe.

18. RADIO RADIO (Costello)/TINY STEPS (Costello)
UK Radar ADA 24.
Released October 1978.
Produced by Nick Lowe.
    Highest UK chart placing: 29.

20. TALKING IN THE DARK (Costello)/WEDNESDAY WEEK (Costello)
UK Radar RG 1.
Released December 1978.
Produced by Nick Lowe.
    Given away at London Dominion Christmas shows 1978, and three New York shows January 1979.

19. AMERICAN SQUIRM (Lowe)/(WHAT'S SO FUNNY 'BOUT) PEACE, LOVE AND UNDERSTANDING (Lowe)
UK Radar ADA 26.
Released October 1978.
Produced by Nick Lowe.
    A-side performed by Nick Lowe. Although credited to 'Nick Lowe And His Sound', B-side is in fact Elvis Costello and The Attractions.

21. OLIVER'S ARMY (Costello)/MY FUNNY VALENTINE (Rodgers and Hart)
UK Radar ADA 31.
Released February 1979.
Produced by Nick Lowe.
    Highest UK chart placing: 2.

SINGLES

22. Elvis Costello And The Attractions – LIVE AT HOLLYWOOD HIGH: ACCIDENTS WILL HAPPEN (Costello) Live/ALISON (Costello) Live/WATCHING THE DETECTIVES (Costello) Live
UK Radar SAM 90.
US Columbia AE7-1171.
Released February 1979.

Free with initial batches of 'Armed Forces' album. Sleeve has 'Adcidents (sic) Will Happen'. US version has slightly different timings.

24. OLIVER'S ARMY (Costello)/MY FUNNY VALENTINE (Rodgers and Hart)
JAP Radar P-387F.
Released March 1979.
Produced by Nick Lowe.

23. MY FUNNY VALENTINE (Rodgers and Hart)/(WHAT'S SO FUNNY 'BOUT) PEACE, LOVE AND UNDERSTANDING (Lowe)
US Columbia AE7-1172.
Released February 1979.
Produced by Nick Lowe.

Promo only, red vinyl with floating hearts label. Also copies in heart-shaped red vinyl. Given away at St. Valentine's Day gig, Long Beach, California.

25. ACCIDENTS WILL HAPPEN (Costello)/TALKING IN THE DARK (Costello)/WEDNESDAY WEEK (Costello)
UK Radar ADA 35.
GER RAD 17 393N.
Released May 1979.
Produced by Nick Lowe.

Three different UK picture sleeves – standard design with artwork as for the promo video, reversed sleeve with the same artwork but on the inside, and a 'Fish Is Brain Food' picture which was possibly an earlier discarded design.

Highest UK chart placing: 28.

26. ACCIDENTS WILL HAPPEN (Costello)/SUNDAY'S BEST (Costello)
US Columbia 3-10919.
Released 1979.
Produced by Nick Lowe.

27. ACCIDENTS WILL HAPPEN (Costello)/TALKING IN THE DARK (Costello)/WEDNESDAY WEEK (Costello)
JAP Radar P-444F.
Released July 1979.
Produced by Nick Lowe.
   Sleeve is also a variation on the 'inside out' idea with full artwork on the inside.

28. I CAN'T STAND UP FOR FALLING DOWN (Homer Banks, Allan Jones)/GIRLS TALK (Costello)
UK Two-Tone TT 7.
NOT released January 1980.
Produced by Nick Lowe.
   Release was prevented by court writ, but copies were given away some time later at a London Rainbow concert.

29. I CAN'T STAND UP FOR FALLING DOWN (Homer Banks, Allan Jones)/GIRLS TALK (Costello)
UK F-Beat XX1.
US Columbia 1-11194.
HOL F-Beat WEA 18171.
Released January 1980.
Produced by Nick Lowe.
   Sleeve has B-side title as 'Girl's Talk'.
   Highest UK chart placing: 4.

30. I CAN'T STAND UP FOR FALLING DOWN (Homer Banks, Allan Jones)/GIRLS TALK (Costello)/SECONDARY MODERN (Costello)/KING HORSE (Costello)
US Columbia 1-11251.
Released 1980.
Produced by Nick Lowe.

31. I CAN'T STAND UP FOR FALLING DOWN (Homer Banks, Allan Jones)/GIRLS TALK (Costello)
JAP F-Beat P-551X.
Released March 1980.
Produced by Nick Lowe.

32. HIGH FIDELITY (Costello)/ GETTING MIGHTY CROWDED (Van McCoy)
UK F-Beat XX3.
Released April 1980.
Produced by Nick Lowe.
Highest UK chart placing: 30.

34. NEW AMSTERDAM (Costello)/ DR. LUTHER'S ASSISTANT (Costello)
UK F-Beat XX5.
Released June 1980.
Produced by Nick Lowe.
B-side produced by Costello.
Budget priced companion to the 'New Amsterdam' EP

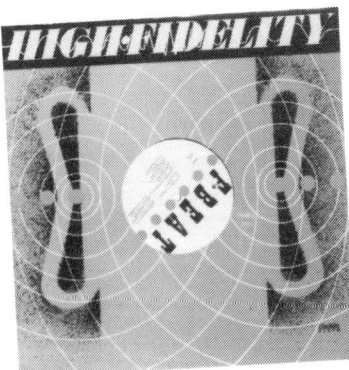

33. HIGH FIDELITY (Costello)/ GETTING MIGHTY CROWDED (Van McCoy)/CLOWNTIME IS OVER (Costello) Version 2.
UK F-Beat XX3T (12" Single).
Released April 1980.
Produced by Nick Lowe.
12" version of the above, with extra track different to the album version.

SINGLES

**35. NEW AMSTERDAM (Costello)/
DR. LUTHER'S ASSISTANT
(Costello)/GHOST TRAIN (Costello)/
JUST A MEMORY (Costello)**
UK F-Beat XX5E.
UK F-Beat XX5P (picture disc).
HOL F-Beat WEA 18288.
Released June 1980.
'New Amsterdam' produced by Nick
Lowe, other tracks produced by Elvis
Costello.

First 1,500 picture discs issued with
black rim, later copies with transparent
rim.

Highest UK chart placing: 36.

**37. NEW AMSTERDAM (Costello)/
DR. LUTHER'S ASSISTANT
(Costello)/GHOST TRAIN (Costello)/
JUST A MEMORY (Costello)**
JAP F-Beat P-615X.
Released September 1980.
'New Amsterdam' produced by Nick
Lowe, other tracks produced by Elvis
Costello.

**38. NEW AMSTERDAM (Costello)/
WEDNESDAY WEEK (Costello)**
US Columbia 1-11284.
Released 1980.
Produced by Nick Lowe.

**36. HIGH FIDELITY (Costello)/
GETTING MIGHTY CROWDED
(Van McCoy)**
JAP F-Beat P-585X.
Released June 1980.
A-side produced by Nick Lowe, B-side
produced by Elvis Costello.

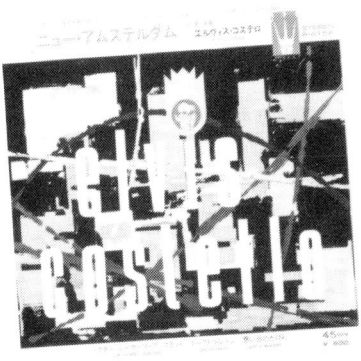

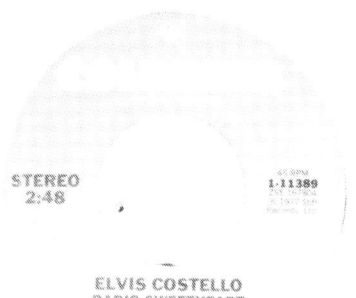

**39. GETTING MIGHTY CROWDED
(Van McCoy)/RADIO SWEETHEART
(Costello)**
US Columbia 1-11389.
Released 1980.
A-side produced by Elvis Costello, B-side
produced by Nick Lowe.

40. CLUBLAND (Costello)/CLEAN MONEY (Costello)/HOOVER FACTORY (Costello)
UK F-Beat XX12.
Released December 1980.
Produced by Nick Lowe, except 'Hoover Factory' produced by Elvis Costello, and also credited as a solo recording.
  Highest UK chart placing: 60.

41. FOUR TRACKS FROM THE 'TRUST' LP: YOU'LL NEVER BE A MAN (Costello)/PRETTY WORDS (Costello)/FROM A WHISPER TO A SCREAM (Costello)/NEW LACE SLEEVES (Costello)
UK F-Beat.
Released January 1981.
Produced by Nick Lowe in association with Roger Bechirian.
  12" promo release only.

42. 'ELVIS COSTELLO' – Stiff singles four-pack: Includes LESS THAN ZERO (Stiff BUY 11)/ ALISON (Stiff BUY 14)/RED SHOES (Stiff BUY 15)/WATCHING THE DETECTIVES (Stiff BUY 20)
UK Stiff GRAB 3.
Released 1981.
All tracks produced by Nick Lowe.
  A re-issue of the four Stiff singles in their original sleeves (except of course for 'Red Shoes') and in a special wallet. Slight label differences are sufficient to distinguish these from the originals, notably 'Made In England' and 'Ltd.' after (C). Stiff Records no longer appears on these.

43. CLUBLAND (Costello)/CLEAN MONEY (Costello)/HOOVER FACTORY (Costello)
JAP F-Beat P-1505X.
Released February 1981.
Produced by Nick Lowe, except for 'Hoover Factory' produced by Elvis Costello, and also credited as a solo recording.

44. WATCH YOUR STEP (Costello)/ LUXEMBOURG (Costello)
US Columbia 11-60519.
Released 1981.
Produced by Nick Lowe.

45. WATCH YOUR STEP (Costello)/ TOM SNYDER INTERVIEW (2.4.81)
US Columbia AS 958.
Released 1981.
A-side produced by Nick Lowe.
  12" promo release only.

46. FROM A WHISPER TO A SCREAM (Costello)/LUXEMBOURG (Costello)
UK F-Beat XX14.
Released February 1981.
Produced by Nick Lowe, in association with Roger Bechirian.
　A-side has Glenn Tilbrook from Squeeze as guest vocalist.

47. FROM A WHISPER TO A SCREAM (Costello)/LUXEMBOURG (Costello)
SPAIN F-Beat CP 369.
Released 1981.
Produced by Nick Lowe, in association with Roger Bechirian.
　A-side Glenn Tilbrook guest vocalist.
7" promo release only.

48. ALISON (Costello)/ACCIDENTS WILL HAPPEN (Costello)
US Columbia Hall Of Fame 13-33401.
Released 1981.
Produced by Nick Lowe.
　Re-released as part of the 'Hall Of Fame' series.

49. GOOD YEAR FOR THE ROSES (Jerry Chesnut)/YOUR ANGEL STEPS OUT OF HEAVEN (Jack Ripley)
UK F-Beat XX17.
HOL F-Beat WEA 18.879.
Released UK September 1981.
Produced by Billy Sherrill.
　UK release in plain white or '45 RPM' sleeve, but no real picture sleeve. Picture sleeve illustrated is Dutch copy.
　Highest UK chart placing: 6.

50. GOOD YEAR FOR THE ROSES (Jerry Chesnut)/COLOUR OF THE BLUES (Williams Jones)/WHY DON'T YOU LOVE ME (LIKE YOU USED TO DO) (Williams)/SWEET DREAMS (Gibson)
UK F-Beat XX17DJ.
Released October 1981.
Produced by Billy Sherrill.
　7" promo release only.

SINGLES

51. A GOOD YEAR FOR THE ROSES (Jerry Chesnut)/A GOOD YEAR FOR THE ROSES (Jerry Chesnut)
US Columbia 18-02629.
Released 1981.
Produced by Billy Sherrill.
7" promo release.

53. I'M YOUR TOY (Etheridge, Parsons) Live/CRY CRY CRY (J. Cash)/WONDERING (J. Werner)
UK F-Beat XX21.
Released April 1982.
A-side recorded live at the Royal Albert Hall, London January 7, 1982, with the Royal Philharmonic Orchestra. Arranged and conducted by Robert Kirby. Other two tracks recorded by Billy Sherrill in Nashville. All tracks mixed by Elvis Costello and Paul Bass.
Highest UK chart placing: 51.

52. SWEET DREAMS (Don Gibson)/PSYCHO (Leon Payne) Live
UK F-Beat XX19.
Released December 1981.
A-side produced by Billy Sherrill. B-side produced by Elvis Costello, recorded live at the Palomino Club, North Hollywood, USA, February 16, 1979.
Highest UK chart placing: 42.

54. I'M YOUR TOY (Etheridge, Parsons) Live/MY SHOES KEEP WALKING BACK TO YOU (Ross, Wills)/BLUES KEEP CALLING (Janis Martin)/HONKY TONK GIRL (Loretta Lynn)
UK F-Beat XX21T (12" Single).
Released April 1982.
Credits for 'I'm Your Toy' are as for No. 53 above. Other tracks recorded by Billy Sherrill in Nashville, mixed by Elvis Costello and Paul Bass in Shepherds Bush, London.

55. YOU LITTLE FOOL (Costello)/ BIG SISTER (Costello)/THE STAMPING GROUND (Costello)
UK F-Beat XX26.
Released June 1982.
'You Little Fool' produced by Geoff Emerick from an original idea by Elvis Costello. 'Big Sister' produced by Nick Lowe. 'The Stamping Ground' produced by Elvis Costello and is credited to 'The Emotional Toothpaste'.

The latter title is listed on the sleeve as 'Stamping Ground!'

Highest UK chart placing: 52.

57. MAN OUT OF TIME (Costello)/ TOWN CRYER (Costello) Alternate version/IMPERIAL BEDROOM (Costello)
UK F-Beat XX28T (12" Single).
Released July 1982.
First two tracks produced by Geoff Emerick from an original idea by Elvis Costello. 'Imperial Bedroom' produced by Elvis Costello and credited to 'Napoleon Dynamite and The Royal Guard'(!).

Issued in a special price limited edition.

56. MAN OUT OF TIME (Costello)/ TOWN CRYER (Costello) Alternate version
UK F-Beat XX28.
Released July 1982.
Produced by Geoff Emerick from an original idea by Elvis Costello.
Highest UK chart placing: 58.

58. MAN OUT OF TIME (Costello) DJ edit/ELVIS COSTELLO INTRODUCES MAN OUT OF TIME/ MAN OUT OF TIME (Costello)
UK F-Beat XX28DJ.
Released July 1982.
Produced by Geoff Emerick from an original idea by Elvis Costello.

DJ edit is a 3'57" version. Introduction is taken from the 'A Conversation With Elvis Costello' promo interview double album. This is a 7" promo only release.

**59. MAN OUT OF TIME (Costello)/
MAN OUT OF TIME (Costello)**
US Columbia 18-03202.
Released July 1982.
Produced by Geoff Emerick.
   Double A-side promo release.

60. MAN OUT OF TIME (Costello)
US Columbia CNR-03269.
Released July 1982.
Produced by Geoff Emerick.
   A one-sided single, aimed at reducing the price of singles – it didn't catch on!

**61. MAN OUT OF TIME (Costello)/
BEYOND BELIEF (Costello)**
US Columbia AS 1510.
Released July 1982.
Produced by Geoff Emerick.
   12" promo release only.

62. HOMBRE DESFASADO (MAN OUT OF TIME) (Costello)/TOWN CRYER (Costello) Alternate version
SPAIN F-Beat WEA 24 9983-7.
Released July 1982.
Produced by Geoff Emerick.
   Despite the title, A-side is not sung in Spanish.

63. FROM HEAD TO TOE (Robinson)/THE WORLD OF BROKEN HEARTS (Pomus, Shuman)
UK F-Beat XX30.
Released September 1982.
Produced by Elvis Costello assisted by Paul Bass.
   A limited edition with free 'Get Happy!' album (!) caused a 'chart hype' furore.
   Highest UK chart placing: 43.

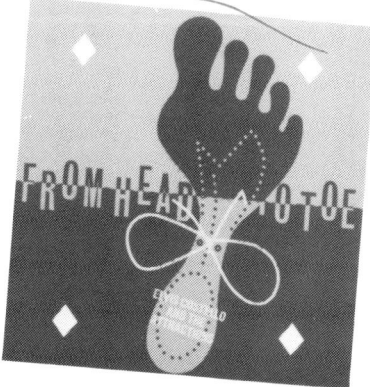

**64. PARTY PARTY (Costello)/
IMPERIAL BEDROOM (Costello)**
UK A&M AMS 8267.
Released November 1982.
A-side produced by Elvis Costello and Colin Fairley, B-side produced by Elvis Costello.
   Both sides with The Royal Guard Horns. A-side from the soundtrack to 'Party Party' – see under compilations.
   Highest UK chart placing: 48.

65. Elvis Costello And The Attractions: PARTY PARTY (Costello)/ NO FEELINGS (Matlock/ Rotten/Cook/Jones)
UK A&M PARTY 5.
Released November 1982.
  A-side with The Royal Guard Horns, produced by Elvis Costello and Colin Fairley.
  B-side performed by Bananarama.
  7" promo only release for 'Party Party' soundtrack.

67. EVERYDAY I WRITE THE BOOK (Costello)/HEATHEN TOWN (Costello)
UK F-Beat XX32.
Released June 1983.
Produced by Clive Langer and Alan Winstanley.
  First release through new distribution deal with RCA in the UK.
  Highest UK chart placing: 28.

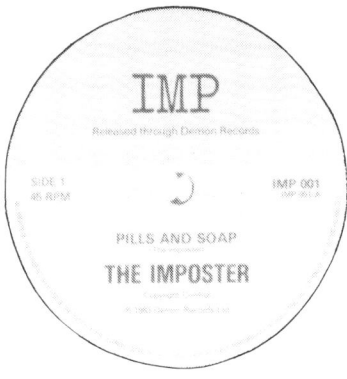

66. The Imposter: PILLS AND SOAP (The Imposter)/PILLS AND SOAP (The Imposter) Extended version
UK IMP Records IMP 001.
Released May 1983.
Produced by Fairley/Imposter.
  Written, recorded and co-produced by Elvis Costello, this was issued in a limited edition under 'The Imposter' due to legal wrangles over a new UK record contract.
  Highest UK chart placing: 16.

68. EVERYDAY I WRITE THE BOOK (Costello)/HEATHEN TOWN (Costello)/NIGHT TIME (Chambers)
UK F-Beat XX32T (12" Single).
Released June 1983.
Produced by Clive Langer and Alan Winstanley, except 'Night Time' produced by Elvis Costello, assisted by Paul Bass.
  Original 3'54" version (same as 7") was quickly withdrawn and replaced by 4'25" extended remix version of 'Everyday I Write The Book', but with no change to the sleeve.

69. EVERYDAY I WRITE THE BOOK (Costello)/HEATHEN TOWN (Costello)
US Columbia 38-04045.
Released August 1983.
Produced by Clive Langer and Alan Winstanley.

71. LET THEM ALL TALK (Costello)/ THE FLIRTING KIND (Costello)
UK F-Beat XX33.
Released September 1983.
Produced by Clive Langer and Alan Winstanley.
  A-side with the TKO Horns.
  Highest UK chart placing: 59.

70. EVERYDAY I WRITE THE BOOK (Costello) Extended remix/ EVERYDAY I WRITE THE BOOK (Costello) Instrumental/HEATHEN TOWN (Costello)/NIGHT TIME (Chambers)
US Columbia 44-04115.
Released August 1983.
Produced by Clive Langer and Alan Winstanley, except 'Night Time' produced by Elvis Costello, assisted by Paul Bass.
  This remix of 'Everyday' is even longer at 5'04", 'Special Club Version' mixed by John 'Jellybean' Benitez and John 'Tokes' Potoker. Instrumental is 3'40".

72. LET THEM ALL TALK (Costello)/ THE FLIRTING KIND (Costello)
UK F-Beat XX33T (12" Single).
Released September 1983.
Produced by Clive Langer and Alan Winstanley.
  A-side is extended remix (5'59"), with the TKO Horns.

73. LET THEM ALL TALK (Costello)/ LET THEM ALL TALK (Costello)
US Columbia 38-04266 (ZSS 171500).
Released September 1983.
Produced by Clive Langer and Alan Winstanley.
  Double A-sided 7" US promo release only.

74. LET THEM ALL TALK (Costello)/ SHIPBUILDING (Costello, C. Langer)
US Columbia 38-04266 (ZSS 171501).
Released September 1983.
Produced by Clive Langer and Alan Winstanley.

75. LET THEM ALL TALK (Costello)/ THE FLIRTING KIND (Costello)
FRANCE F-Beat PC 61277 (12" Single).
Released 1983.
Produced by Clive Langer and Alan Winstanley.
  A-side is extended remix.

76. SHIPBUILDING (Costello)/ THE WORLD AND HIS WIFE (Costello)
Jap F-Beat RPS 118.
Released 1984.

77. The Imposter: PEACE IN OUR TIME (The Imposter)/WITHERED AND DIED (Richard Thompson)
UK Imposter Records TRUCE 1.
Released April 1984.
A-side produced by Clive Langer and Alan Winstanley. B-side produced by Fairley/Imposter.
  Released under 'The Imposter' title to denote a separate solo project from recordings with The Attractions.
  Highest UK chart placing: 48.

78. I WANNA BE LOVED (Farnell/ Jenkins)/TURNING THE TOWN RED (Costello)
UK F-Beat XX35.
Released June 1984.

79. I WANNA BE LOVED (Farnell/ Jenkins)/TURNING THE TOWN RED (Costello)/I WANNA BE LOVED (Extended version) (Costello)
UK F-Beat XX35T (12" single).
Released June 1984.

SINGLES

ALBUMS

WORLDWIDE

1. MY AIM IS TRUE
UK Stiff SEEZ 3.
FRANCE Stiff SRL 910.010.
FRANCE Stiff SEEZ 3NP, reissue.
JAP Stiff VIP-6581.
Released July 1977.
Produced by Nick Lowe.
Recorded at Pathway Studios, Highbury, N. London.

Side One: 1. Welcome To The Working Week (Costello)/2. Miracle Man (Costello)/3. No Dancing (Costello)/4. Blame It On Cain (Costello)/5. Alison (Costello)/6. Sneaky Feelings (Costello).

Side Two: 7. (The Angels Wanna Wear My) Red Shoes (Costello)/8. Less Than Zero (Costello)/9. Mystery Dance (Costello)/10. Pay It Back (Costello)/11. I'm Not Angry (Costello)/12. Waiting For The End Of The World (Costello).

Elvis Costello guitar, vocals. John McFee guitar, vocals. Huey Louis harmonica, vocals. Johnny Ciambotti bass, vocals. Sean Hopper keyboards, vocals. Alex Call guitar, vocals. Micky Shine drums, vocals.

Sleeve photos by Keith Morris. Up to eleven different shades have been used on the sleeve, but there were only four different ones to start with! In 1978 the front sleeve photo was 'cleaned up' in line with the US release.

Matrix note 'Elvis Is King' and 'On This Side Too'.

Highest UK chart placing: 10.

ALBUMS

2. MY AIM IS TRUE
US Columbia AL 35037.
Released March 1978.
Produced by Nick Lowe.
Recorded at Pathway Studios, Highbury, N. London.

Side One: 1. Welcome To The Working Week (Costello)/2. Miracle Man (Costello)/3. No Dancing (Costello)/ 4. Blame It On Cain (Costello)/5. Alison (Costello)/6. Sneaky Feelings (Costello)/ 7. Watching The Detectives (Costello).

Side Two: 8. (The Angels Wanna Wear My) Red Shoes (Costello)/9. Less Than Zero (Costello)/10. Mystery Dance (Costello)/11. Pay It Back (Costello)/ 12. I'm Not Angry (Costello)/13. Waiting For The End Of The World (Costello).

Musicians' credits same as for No. 1 above.

Sleeve photos by Keith Morris. This release was the first to feature the 'cleaned up' front sleeve photo, later also adopted for No. 1 above. No variation in colours used – all yellow.

3. THIS YEAR'S MODEL
UK Radar RAD 3.
JAP Radar P-10538F.
Released March 1978.
Produced by Nick Lowe.

Side One: 1. No Action (Costello)/ 2. This Year's Girl (Costello)/3. The Beat (Costello)/4. Pump It Up (Costello)/5. Little Triggers (Costello)/6. You Belong To Me (Costello).

Side Two: 7. Hand In Hand (Costello)/8. (I Don't Want To Go To) Chelsea (Costello)/9. Lip Service (Costello)/10. Living In Paradise (Costello)/ 11. Lipstick Vogue (Costello)/12. Night Rally (Costello).

Elvis Costello guitar, vocals. Steve Naive keyboards. Bruce Thomas bass. Pete Thomas drums.

Intentionally non-aligned sleeve with different front and back sleeve photos, and inner sleeve 'portable TV' photo, to either the US or European releases. The UK sleeve was 'correctly' lined up when the album was re-issued on F-Beat XXLP 4 in 1980 following the collapse of Radar.

Matrix note on initial copies 'Special pressing No. 003. Ring Moira on 434-3232 for your special prize'. It was a joke and '003' was the only number used – Moira was press officer at WEA and was inundated with phone calls.

Reissued UK on IMP Records FIEND 18, April, 1984.

Highest UK chart placing: 4.

4. THIS YEAR'S MODEL
SWEDEN Smash SLEPT 2.
FRANCE Radar 56 447.
Released March 1978.
Produced by Nick Lowe.

Side One: 1. No Action (Costello)/
2. This Year's Girl (Costello)/3. The
Beat (Costello)/4. Pump It Up (Costello)/
5. Little Triggers (Costello)/6. You Belong
To Me (Costello)/7. Watching The
Detectives (Costello).
 Side Two: 8. Hand In Hand
(Costello)/9. (I Don't Want To Go To)
Chelsea (Costello)/10. Lip Service
(Costello)/11. Living In Paradise (Costello)/
12. Lipstick Vogue (Costello)/13. Night
Rally (Costello).
 Musicians' credits same as for No. 3
above.
 Featured lined-up sleeve, with different
inner and outer sleeve photos as
mentioned above.

5. THIS YEAR'S MODEL
US Columbia JC 35331.
Released May 1978.
Produced by Nick Lowe.
 Reissued in the Columbia mid-price
range as PC-35331 March 1984.
 Side One: 1. No Action (Costello)/
2. This Year's Girl(Costello)/3. The Beat
(Costello)/4. Pump It Up (Costello)/5. Little
Triggers (Costello)/6. You Belong To Me
(Costello).
 Side Two: 7. Hand In Hand
(Costello)/8. Lip Service (Costello)/
9. Living In Paradise (Costello)/10. Lipstick
Vogue (Costello)/11. Radio Radio
(Costello).
 Musicians' credits same as for No. 3
above.
 Apart from yet another track listing,
this has a lined up sleeve, and alternative
inner and outer sleeve photos to either
No. 3 or No. 4 above. Also issued as a
picture disc.

6. LIVE AT THE EL MOCAMBO
CANADA Columbia CDN-10C.
Released 1978.
 Side One: Mystery Dance (Costello)/
2. Waiting For The End Of The World
(Costello)/3. Welcome To The Working
Week (Costello)/4. Less Than Zero
(Costello) Dallas version/5. The Beat
(Costello)/6. Lip Service (Costello)/
7. Chelsea (Costello)/8. Little Triggers
(Costello)/9. Radio Radio (Costello).
 Side Two: 10. Lipstick Vogue
(Costello)/11. Watching The Detectives
(Costello)/12. Miracle Man (Costello)/
13. You Belong To Me (Costello)/
14. Pump It Up (Costello).
 Elvis Costello guitar, vocals. Steve
Naive keyboards. Bruce Thomas bass.
Pete Thomas drums. Martin Belmont
rhythm guitar.
 A live promotional album distributed
in Canada without permission from
Elvis or Jake, this has been widely
counterfeited and bootlegged. Original
pressing was for 500 copies only.

7. ARMED FORCES
UK Radar RAD 14.
Released February 1979.
Produced by Nick Lowe.
 Side One: 1. Accidents Will Happen
(Costello)/2. Senior Service (Costello)/
3. Oliver's Army (Costello)/4. Big Boys
(Costello)/5. Green Shirt (Costello)/
6. Party Girl (Costello).
 Side Two: 7. Goon Squad (Costello)/
8. Busy Bodies (Costello)/9. Sunday's
Best (Costello)/10. Moods For Moderns
(Costello)/11. Chemistry Class (Costello)/
12. Two Little Hitlers (Costello).
 Elvis Costello guitar, vocals. Steve
Naive keyboards. Bruce Thomas bass.
Pete Thomas drums.
 Original UK sleeve opened out
completely and included a set of
postcards – this was later switched to the
more conventional format. Initial copies

included a free 'Live At Hollywood High' E.P. with tracks: Accidents Will Happen (Costello), Alison (Costello), and Watching The Detectives (Costello) – see Singles Section No. 22.

Reissued on F-Beat XXLP5 5 in 1980 following the collapse of Radar.

Reissued UK on IMP Records FIEND 21. April, 1984.

Highest UK chart placing: 2.

8. ARMED FORCES
US Columbia JC 35709.
JAP Radar P-10627F.
FRANCE Radar 35 709.
Released February 1979.
Produced by Nick Lowe.

Side One: 1. Accidents Will Happen (Costello)/2. Senior Service (Costello)/ 3. Oliver's Army (Costello)/4. Big Boys (Costello)/5. Green Shirt (Costello)/ 6. Party Girl (Costello).

Side Two: 7. Goon Squad (Costello)/ 8. Busy Bodies (Costello)/9. Moods For Moderns (Costello)/10. Chemistry Class (Costello)/11. Two Little Hitlers (Costello)/ 12. (What's So Funny 'Bout) Peace, Love And Understanding (Lowe).

Elvis Costello guitar, vocals. Steve Naive keyboards. Bruce Thomas bass. Pete Thomas drums.

Different sleeve to the UK, utilising the inner artwork for the front and transferring the 'elephants' artwork to the rear. Initial copies also included the free 'Live At Hollywood High' EP – see Singles Section No. 22.

9. GET HAPPY!!
UK F-Beat XXLP 1.
US Columbia JC 36347.
JAP F-Beat P-10804X.
FRANCE F-Beat 36 347.
Released March 1980.

Produced by Nick Lowe, balanced by Roger Bechirian.
Recorded in Holland.

Side One: 1. Love For Tender (Costello)/2. Opportunity (Costello)/3. The Imposter (Costello)/4. Secondary Modern (Costello)/5. King Horse (Costello)/6. Possession (Costello)/7. Man Called Uncle (Costello)/8. Clowntime Is Over (Costello)/9. New Amsterdam (Costello)/ 10. High Fidelity (Costello).

Side Two: 11. I Can't Stand Up For Falling Down (H. Banks, A. Jones)/ 12. Black And White World (Costello)/ 13. Five Gears In Reverse (Costello)/ 14. B Movie (Costello)/15. Motel Matches (Costello)/16. Human Touch (Costello)/ 17. Beaten To The Punch (Costello)/ 18. Temptation (Costello)/19. I Stand Accused (T. Colton, R. Smith)/20. Riot Act (Costello).

Elvis Costello guitar, vocals. Steve Naive keyboards. Bruce Thomas bass. Pete Thomas drums.

The first Costello album not to have some variation on the track listing issued somewhere in the world. There is however a difference in the sleeve artwork. The UK sleeve has a novel 'preworn' look, but this was removed for release in other countries. Sleeve has track listing for sides one and two reversed.

Reissued UK on IMP Records FIEND 24. April, 1984.

Highest UK chart placing: 2.

10. GET HAPPY!!
UK F-Beat XXPROMO 1.
Released March 1980.
Produced by Nick Lowe, balanced by Roger Bechirian.
Recorded in Holland.

Side One: 1. Love For Tender (Costello)/2. Opportunity (Costello)/3. The Imposter (Costello)/4. Secondary Modern (Costello)/5. King Horse (Costello).
Side Two: 6. Possession (Costello)/ 7. Man Called Uncle (Costello)/ 8. Clowntime Is Over (Costello)/9. New Amsterdam (Costello)/10. High Fidelity (Costello).
Side Three: 11. I Can't Stand Up For Falling Down (H. Banks, A. Jones)/ 12. Black And White World (Costello)/ 13. Five Gears In Reverse (Costello)/ 14. B Movie (Costello)/15. Motel Matches (Costello).
Side Four: 16. Human Touch (Costello)/17. Beaten To The Punch (Costello)/18. Temptation (Costello)/ 19. I Stand Accused (T. Colton, R. Smith)/ 20. Riot Act (Costello).
Elvis Costello guitar, vocals. Steve Naive keyboards. Bruce Thomas bass. Pete Thomas drums.
Two records at 45 rpm covering all 20 songs from the album, five to a side. Double promo black and white cover with F-Beat logo, also includes 8" x 10" still and album poster.

Side Two: 11. Getting Mighty Crowded (Van McCoy) produced by Costello/ 12. Hoover Factory (Costello) produced by Costello/13. Tiny Steps (Costello)/ 14. (I Don't Want To Go To) Chelsea (Costello)/15. Dr. Luther's Assistant (Costello) produced by Costello/ 16. Sunday's Best (Costello)/ 17. Crawling To The U.S.A. (Costello) produced by Costello/18. Wednesday Week (Costello)/19. My Funny Valentine (Rodgers & Hart) produced by Costello/ 20. Ghost Train (Costello) produced by Costello.
Elvis Costello guitar, vocals. Steve Nieve (note name change) keyboards. Bruce Thomas bass. Pete Thomas drums. Elvis with Clover on 'Radio Sweetheart' and 'Stranger In The House'. Guest appearances from Dave Edmunds and Mick Jones.
A collection of some of the rarer tracks not otherwise on album. Sleeve design by CBS Records Art Department. Front sleeve photo is intentionally back to front. A-side label has 'Costello' instead of 'Columbia'.

11. TAKING LIBERTIES
US Columbia JC 36839.
FRANCE Columbia 36 839.
Released November 1980.
Produced by Nick Lowe, except where noted.
Side One: 1. Clean Money (Costello)/ 2. Girls Talk (Costello)/3. Talking In The Dark (Costello)/4. Radio Sweetheart (Costello)/5. Black And White World (Costello) produced by Costello/6. Big Tears (Costello)/7. Just A Memory (Costello) produced by Costello/ 8. Night Rally (Costello)/9. Stranger In The House (Costello)/10. Clowntime Is Over (Costello) produced by Costello.

12. TAKING LIBERTIES
US Columbia AS 847.
Released November 1980.
Promotional 12" release only.
Clean Money (Costello), Radio Sweetheart (Costello), Getting Mighty Crowded (Van McCoy), Talking In The Dark (Costello). All tracks taken from No. 11 above.

13. TEN BLOODY MARYS AND TEN HOW'S YOUR FATHERS
UK F-Beat XXC 6 (Cassette only release).
Released November 1980.
Produced by Nick Lowe, except where noted.

Side One: 1. Clean Money (Costello)/
2. Girls Talk (Costello)/3. Talking In The
Dark (Costello)/4. Radio Sweetheart
(Costello)/5. Big Tears (Costello)/
6. Crawling To The U.S.A. (Costello)
produced by Costello/7. Just A Memory
(Costello) produced by Costello/
8. Watching The Detectives (Costello)/
9. Stranger In The House (Costello)/
10. Clowntime Is Over (Costello)
produced by Costello.
Side Two: 11. Getting Mighty Crowded
(Van McCoy) produced by Costello/
12. Hoover Factory (Costello) produced
by Costello/13. Tiny Steps (Costello)/
14. (What's So Funny 'Bout) Peace,
Love And Understanding (Lowe)/
15. Dr. Luther's Assistant (Costello)
produced by Costello/16. Radio Radio
(Costello)/17. Black And White World
(Costello) produced by Costello/
18. Wednesday Week (Costello)/
19. My Funny Valentine (Rodgers & Hart)
produced by Costello/20. Ghost Train
(Costello) produced by Costello.

Elvis Costello guitar, vocals. Steve
Nieve keyboards. Bruce Thomas bass.
Pete Thomas drums. Elvis with Clover on
'Radio Sweetheart' and 'Stranger In The
House'. Guest appearances from Dave
Edmunds and Mick Jones.

UK equivalent release to 'Taking
Liberties', with the changes necessary
because of the variation of tracks on the
earlier album releases. Issued as a
limited edition cassette-only release, in a
'gold'-plated cassette and cassette case.
Also a 6-track 7" promo (EL-1). See also
Album Section listing No. 21.

Produced by Nick Lowe, in association
with Roger Bechirian, assisted by Neil
King. 'Big Sister's Clothes' produced by
Elvis Costello.
Side One: 1. Clubland (Costello)/
2. Lover's Walk (Costello)/3. You'll Never
Be A Man (Costello)/4. Pretty Words
(Costello)/5. Strict Time (Costello)/
6. Luxembourg (Costello)/7. Watch Your
Step (Costello).
Side Two: 8. New Lace Sleeves
(Costello)/9. From A Whisper To A
Scream (Costello)/10. Different Finger
(Costello)/11. White Knuckles (Costello)/
12. Shot With His Own Gun (Costello)/
13. Fish 'n' Chip Paper (Costello)/14. Big
Sister's Clothes (Costello).

Elvis Costello guitar, vocals. Steve
Nieve keyboards. Bruce Thomas bass.
Pete Thomas drums. Martin Belmont
guitar. Glenn Tilbrook featured vocalist
on 'From A Whisper To A Scream'.

Reissued UK on IMP Records
FIEND 30. April, 1984.

Highest UK chart placing: 9.

15. ALMOST BLUE
UK F-Beat XXLP 13.
US Columbia JC 37051.
GER F-Beat FB K 58 392.
FRANCE F-Beat 58 392.
Released October 1981.
Produced by Billy Sherrill in CBS Studio
'A', Nashville May 18-29, 1981.
Engineered by Ron 'Snake' Reynolds,
assisted by Fast Eddy Hudson.
Side One: 1. Why Don't You Love Me
(Like You Used To Do) (Williams)/
2. Sweet Dreams (Gibson)/3. Success
(Mullins)/4. I'm Your Toy (Ethridge)/
5. Tonight The Bottle Let Me Down
(Haggard)/6. Brown To Blue (Jones,
Mathis, Frank).
Side Two: 7. Good Year For The
Roses (Chesnut)/8. Sittin' And Thinkin'
(Rich)/9. Colour Of The Blues (Williams,
Jones)/10. Too Far Gone (Sherrill)/

14. TRUST
UK F-Beat XXLP 11.
US Columbia JC 37051.
GER F-Beat FB 58260.
FRANCE F-Beat 37 051.
SPAIN F-Beat S90.331.
Released January 1981.

11. Honey Hush (Turner)/12. How Much I Lied (Parsons, Rifkin).

Elvis Costello guitar, vocals. Steve Nieve (spelt Neive on the sleeve) piano, organ. Bruce Thomas bass. Pete Thomas drums. Special guest John McFee lead guitar and pedal steel, Nashville Edition backing vocals, Tommy Miller violin.

Apart from the basic blue on the sleeve, four different colour tones were used making four separate sleeves. 'Warning' label states 'This album contains Country and Western music & may produce radical reaction in narrow minded people.'

Reissued UK on IMP Records FIEND 33. April 1984.

Highest UK chart placing: 7.

Elvis Costello guitar, vocals. Steve Nieve keyboards. Bruce Thomas bass. Pete Thomas drums. Special guest John McFee lead guitar and pedal steel. Nashville Edition backing vocals. Tommy Miller violin.

Special individually stamped and numbered sketch cover, each copy with personal autographs from the band.

17. ALMOST NEW
AUSTRALIA F-Beat ELVIS 82.
Released 1982 to coincide with tour.
Side Two produced by Nick Lowe.
Side One: 1. I'm Your Toy (Ethridge, Parsons) Live/2. Accidents Will Happen (Costello) Live/3. Alison (Costello) Live.
Side Two: 4. I Can't Stand Up For Falling Down (H. Banks, A. Jones)/ 5. Green Shirt (Costello)/6. Pump It Up (Costello)/7. (What's So Funny 'Bout) Peace, Love And Understanding (Lowe).

Elvis Costello guitar, vocals. Steve Nieve keyboards. Bruce Thomas bass. Pete Thomas drums.

'I'm Your Toy' live at the Royal Albert Hall, London, January 7, 1982, with the Royal Philharmonic Orchestra. Arranged and conducted by Robert Kirby.

'Accidents Will Happen' and 'Alison' taken from the 'Live At Hollywood High' EP. See Singles Section listing No. 22.

Sleeve design by Geoff Barlow and Philip Mortlock.

16. ELVIS COSTELLO INTRODUCES ... THE TRACKS FROM HIS NEW ALBUM 'ALMOST BLUE'
UK F-Beat E.C.CHAT 1.
US Columbia AS 1318.
Released October 1981.
Produced by Billy Sherrill in CBS Studio 'A', Nashville May 18-29, 1981.
Engineered by Ron 'Snake' Reynolds, assisted by Fast Eddy Hudson.
Side One: 1. Intro – Why Don't You Love Me (Like You Used To Do) (Williams)/2. Intro –Sweet Dreams (Gibson)/3. Intro – Success (Mullins)/ 4. Intro – I'm Your Toy (Ethridge)/5. Intro – Tonight The Bottle Let Me Down (Haggard)/6. Intro – Brown To Blue (Jones, Mathis, Frank).
Side Two: 7. Intro – Good Year For The Roses (Chesnut)/8. Intro – Sittin' And Thinkin' (Rich)/9. Intro – Colour Of The Blues (Williams, Jones)/10. Intro – Too Far Gone (Sherrill)/11. Intro – Honey Hush (Turner)/12. Intro – How Much I Lied (Parsons, Rifkin).

introduction to each track. Sleeve has the same photo as used for the 'Man Out Of Time' single (see Singles Section No. 56) with the title 'A Conversation With Elvis Costello'. Track listing and musicians and production credits same as for No. 17 above.

18. IMPERIAL BEDROOM
UK F-Beat XXLP 17.
US Columbia FC 38157.
FRANCE F-Beat 203 324.
SPAIN F-Beat WEA 58490.
Released June 1982.
Produced by Geoff Emerick from an original idea by Elvis Costello, assisted by John Jacobs.
Recorded at Air Studios, London.
Side One: 1. Beyond Belief (Costello)/ 2. Tears Before Bedtime (Costello)/ 3. Shabby Doll (Costello)/4. The Long Honeymoon (Costello)/5. Man Out Of Time (Costello)/6. Almost Blue (Costello)/ 7. ... And In Every Home (Costello).
Side Two: 8. The Loved Ones (Costello)/9. Human Hands (Costello)/ 10. Kid About It (Costello)/11. Little Savage (Costello)/12. Boy With A Problem (Costello, Difford)/13. Pidgin English (Costello)/14. You Little Fool (Costello)/15. Town Cryer (Costello).
Elvis Costello guitar, vocals. Steve Nieve keyboards. Bruce Thomas bass. Pete Thomas drums.
Orchestrations by Steve Nieve. 'Boy With A Problem' lyrics by Chris Difford, with additional lyrics by Elvis Costello.
Sleeve painting 'Snakecharmer & Reclining Octopus' by Sal Forlenza 1942. Sleeve photography by David Bailey 1982.
Reissued UK on IMP Records FIEND 36. April, 1984.
Highest UK chart placing: 6.

19. A CONVERSATION WITH ELVIS COSTELLO
UK F-Beat E.C.CHAT 2.
Released July 1982.
Promotional double interview album for 'Imperial Bedroom' along the lines of that for 'Almost Blue'. Includes all the tracks on the album with an interview

20. PUNCH THE CLOCK
UK F-Beat XXLP 19.
US Columbia FC 38897.
US Columbia CK 388197 (Compact Disc).
GER F-Beat 25464.
FRANCE F-Beat 25 464.
Released August 1983.
Produced by Clive Langer and Alan Winstanley.
Recorded at Air Studios, London, assisted by Gavin Greenaway and Colin Fairley. Mixed at Genetic Studios, Reading, assisted by Jim Russell. 'Pills And Soap' is a Fairley/Imposter (Costello) original recording, remodelled by Clanger/Winstanley.
Side One: 1. Let Them All Talk (Costello)/2. Everyday I Write The Book (Costello)/3. The Greatest Thing (Costello)/ 4. The Element Within Her (Costello)/ 5. Love Went Mad (Costello)/ 6. Shipbuilding (Costello, C. Langer).
Side Two: 7. TKO (Boxing Day) (Costello)/8. Charm School (Costello)/ 9. The Invisible Man (Costello)/10. Mouth Almighty (Costello)/11. King Of Thieves (Costello)/12. Pills And Soap (Costello)/ 13. The World And His Wife (Costello).
Elvis Costello Ephiphone, Gretsch and Fender guitars, 'One-finger' synclavier and Casiotone. Steve Nieve Bosendorfer piano, Emulator, Fairlight CMI, Vox organ, Hammond organ, synclavier. Bruce Thomas electric Wal bass guitar. Pete Thomas Gretsch drums, Sabian cymbals.

The TKO Horns: Jim Paterson trombone. Jeff Blythe alto, baritone sax, clarinet. Paul Speare tenor sax, flute. Dave Plews trumpet.

Stuart Robson trumpet, flugelhorn on 'The World And His Wife'. Caron Wheeler, Claudia Fontaine backing vocals (Afrodiziak). Chet Baker trumpet solo on 'Shipbuilding'. David Bedford string arrangements. Morris Pert percussion.

Sleeve design by Phil Smee at Waldo's Design. Sleeve photography by Nick Knight.

Highest UK chart placing: 3.

21. TEN BLOODY MARYS AND TEN HOW'S YOUR FATHERS
UK IMP Records FIEND 27.
Released April 1984.

Identical tracks and credits to the cassette-only version, but released for the first time on album when all the (WEA) F-Beat back-catalogue was transferred to IMP Records.

Sleeve by Phil Smee at Waldo's Design. Photo by Chalkie Davies.

See also Album Section listing No. 13.

22. GOODBYE CRUEL WORLD
UK F-Beat ZL70317.
Released June 1984.
Produced by Clive Langer and Alan Winstanley.
Recorded at Sarm West Studios, London. Assisted by Bob Kraushnar.
Mixed at Genetic Studios, assisted by Jim Russell.

Side One: 1. The Only Flame In Town (Costello)/2. Home Truth (Costello)/ 3. Room With No Number (Costello)/ 4. Inch By Inch (Costello)/5. Worthless Thing (Costello)/6. Love Field (Costello).

Side Two: 1. I Wanna Be Loved (Farnell/Jenkins)/2. The Comedians (Costello)/3. Joe Porterhouse (Costello)/ 4. Sour Milk-Cow Blues (Costello)/5. The Great Unknown (Costello)/6. The Deportees Club (Costello)/7. Peace In Our Time (Costello).

Elvis Costello vocals, guitars and anvil. Maurice Worm Random racket. Bruce Thomas bass guitar. Pete Thomas drums. Gary Barnacle saxes and electric sax. Jim Patterson trombone. Luis Jardim percussion. Daryl Hall and Green backing vocals.

WRITING SONGS FASTER THAN SOME PEOPLE CAN LISTEN.

ELVIS COSTELLO AND THE ATTRACTIONS "GET HAPPY!!" 20 NEW HITS FROM THE ORIGINAL ARTIST. ON COLUMBIA RECORDS AND TAPE.

SOLO EFFORTS
THE ATTRACTIONS

1. SINGLE GIRL (Brain, Hart)/SLOW PATIENCE (B. Thomas, P. Thomas)
(Single).
UK F-Beat XX7.
Released July 1980.
Produced and engineered by Roger Bechirian.

2. ARMS RACE (Nieve)/LONESOME LITTLE TOWNS (B. Thomas, P. Thomas)
(Single).
UK F-Beat XX10.
Released September 1980.
Produced and engineered by Roger Bechirian.

SOLO EFFORTS

3. MAD ABOUT THE WRONG BOY
(LP).
UK F-Beat XXLP 8.
Released September 1980.
Produced and engineered by Roger Bechirian.
　Side One: 1. Arms Race (Nieve)/2. Damage (Nieve)/3. Little Misunderstanding (B. Thomas, P. Thomas)/4. Straight Jacket (Nieve)/5. Mad About The Wrong Boy (Brain, Hart)/6. Motorworld (B. Thomas, P. Thomas)/7. On The Third Stroke (Brain, Hart)/8. Slow Patience (B. Thomas P. Thomas).
　Side Two: 9. La-La-La-La-La Loved You (B. Thomas, P. Thomas)/10. Single Girl (Brain, Hart)/11. Lonesome Little Town (B. Thomas, P. Thomas)/12. Taste Of Poison (Brain, Hart)/13. Highrise Housewife (Brain, Hart)/14. Talk About Me (Nieve)/15. Sad About Girls (Brain, Hart)/16. Camera Camera (Brain, Hart).
　Steve Nieve keyboards. Bruce Thomas bass guitar. Pete Thomas drums. The Attractions vocals and guitars.
　Sleeve photography Brian Griffin. Title on rear of the sleeve is 'Mad About the Rwong Boy'.
　Initial copies included free EP 'Steve Nieve Plays Theme Music From Outline Of A Hairdo'. See listing No. 4 below.
　Reissued UK on IMP Records FIEND 25. April, 1984.

STEVE NIEVE

1. THIS IS YOUR LIFE
The Twist (LP).
UK Polydor 2383 552.
Released 1979.
　Includes Steve Nieve on keyboards.

2. SIX OF ONE AND HALF A DOZEN OF THE OTHER
Howard Werth (LP).
UK Metabop SIXOF 1.
Released 1982.
　Includes Steve Nieve on keyboards.

3. STEVE NIEVE PLAYS THEME MUSIC FROM 'OUTLINE OF A HAIRDO' (Original soundtrack EP)
UK F-Beat COMB 1.
Released September 1980.
　Side One: 1. Outline Of A Hairdo (Nieve)/2. Page One Of A Dead Girl's Diary (Nieve).
　Side Two: 3. Sparrow Crap (Nieve)/4. The Tap Dancer (Nieve).
　Composed and played by Steve Nieve.
　Issued free with initial copies of The Attractions' album 'Mad About The Wrong Boy' – see The Attractions listing No. 3. No separate release.

4. BAD DAY (Paris, Darby, McCourt)/ LAMENT (Paris, Darby, McCourt)
Carmel (Single).
UK London LON 29 (810 143-7).
Released August 1983.
  Includes Steve Nieve on organ.
  B-side performed by Carmel.

5. KEYBOARD JUNGLE
Steve Nieve (LP).
UK Demon Records FIEND 11.
Released December 1983.
Produced by Colin Fairley at Britannia Row, London.
  Side One: 1. The Ethnic Erithian (Nieve)/2. Hooligans And Hula Girls (Nieve)/3. Al Green (Nieve)/4. Spanish Guitar (Nieve)/5. Man With A Musical Lighter (Nieve)/6. Outline Of A Hairdo (Nieve)/7. End Of Side One (Nieve).
  Side Two: 8. Liquid Looks (Nieve)/9. Thought Of Being Dad (Nieve)/10. Pink Flamingoes On Coffee Pot Boulevard (Nieve)/11. The Mystery And Majesty (Of A Banyan Tree) (Nieve)/12. Couch Potato Rag (Nieve)/13. Page One Of A Dead Girl's Diary (Nieve)/14. End Of An Era (Nieve).

Steve Nieve keyboards.
  Sleeve photography by Brian Griffin and David Bailey, artwork by Chimp Carver. Album title Claude Bessy. Sleeve notes by Chris Difford.

6. ONE MINUTE EVERY HOUR (Vanda, Young)/THE THEME FROM 903 (Bradbury)
J.B.'s Allstars (Single).
UK RCA RCA 357 (PB 68098).
Released 1983.
  Includes Steve Nieve on keyboards.

7. BACKFIELD IN MOTION (H.T. McPherson, M. Harden)/ THEME FROM A BEAM (Bradbury)
J.B.'s Allstars (Single).
UK RCA RCA 384 (PB 68135).
Released February 1984.
  Includes Steve Nieve on keyboards.

BRUCE THOMAS

SOLO EFFORTS

1. THE ANSWER
Peter Bardens (LP).
UK Transatlantic TRA 222.
US Verve 3088.
Released 1970.
   Includes Bruce Thomas on bass.

2. QUIVER
Quiver (LP).
UK Warner Bros. K 46089.
US Warner Bros. WB 1939.
Released 1971.
   Includes Bruce Thomas on bass.

3. TIGERS WILL SURVIVE
Ian Matthews (LP).
UK Vertigo 6360 056.
US Vertigo VEL 1010.
Released 1972.
   Includes Bruce Thomas on bass.

4. GONE IN THE MORNING
Quiver (LP).
UK Warner Bros. K46153.
US Warner Bros. WB 2630.
Released 1972.
   Bruce Thomas on bass.

5. THANK YOU FOR
Bridget St. John (LP).
UK Dandelion 2310 193.
Released 1972.
   Includes Bruce Thomas on bass.

6. ORANGE
Al Stewart (LP).
UK CBS CBS 64730.
Released 1972.
   Includes Bruce Thomas on bass.

7. A QUESTION OF ROADS
Mark Ellington (LP).
UK Philips 6308 120.
Released 1972.
   Includes Bruce Thomas on bass.

8. WAIT TILL THEY CHANGE THE BACKDROP
Jonathan Kelly (LP).
UK RCA SF 8353.
Released 1973.
   Includes Bruce Thomas on bass.

9. SHIP IMAGINATION
Billy Lawrie (LP).
UK RCA SF 8395.
Released 1973.
   Includes Bruce Thomas on bass.

10. DREAM KID
Sutherland Brothers & Quiver (LP).
UK Island ILPS 9259.
UK CBS CBS 82299, reissue.
Released 1973.
   Includes Bruce Thomas.

11. PAST, PRESENT AND FUTURE
Al Stewart (LP).
UK CBS CBS 65726.
US Janus 3063.
Released 1974.
   Includes Bruce Thomas on bass.

12. MOONRIDER
Moonrider (LP).
UK Anchor ANCL 2010.
Released 1975.
   Includes Bruce Thomas on bass.

13. QUEENS PARK RANGERS (Thomas)/DRIVE ME DOWN TO QPR (Thomas)
QPR Records QPR 1.
Released 1977.

PETE THOMAS

SOLO EFFORTS

14. BACK TO THE EGG
Paul McCartney & Wings (LP).
UK Parlophone PCTC 257.
Released 1979.
   Includes Bruce Thomas on 'Rockestra' tracks.

15. CONCERTS FOR THE PEOPLE OF KAMPUCHEA
Various Artistes (LP).
UK Atlantic K60153.
US Atlantic 2-7005.
Released March 1981.
   Includes Bruce Thomas on 'Rockestra' tracks.

1. BONGOS OVER BALHAM
Chilli Willi & The Red Hot Peppers (LP).
UK Mooncrest CREST 21.
Released 1974.
   Includes Pete Thomas on drums.

2. JUST POPPED OUT
Sean Tyla & The Tyla Gang (LP).
UK Polydor 2391 463.
US Linegerm 5068.
Released 1980.
   Includes Pete Thomas on drums.

3. STIFFS LIVE STIFFS
Various Artistes (LP).
UK Stiff GET 1.
UK Music For Pleasure MFP.50445, reissue.
Released February 1978.
   Includes Pete Thomas in Larry Wallis' band.

These artists are a bunch of STIFFS

Nick Lowe
Wreckless Eric
Motorhead
Elvis Costello
Magic Michael
Stones Masonry
Jill Read
Dave Edmunds
Tyla Gang
The Takeaways

32 Alexander Street London W2
Reversing into Tomorrow

**A Bunch of Stiffs.
Another great Stiff album**

SPECIAL COLLECTORS ITEM
The first million copies are to be pressed in an attractive black vinyl fi...
The second million will be pressed in gold.

COMPILATIONS

1. EXCERPTS FROM STIFF'S GREATEST HITS
UK Stiff FREEB-2.
Released 1977.
 Promo 7" at 33 rpm includes extracts from Alison/Red Shoes/Watching The Detectives by Elvis Costello. Promotional release.

2. HITS GREATEST STIFFS
UK Stiff FIST 1.
Released 1977.
 Includes 'Radio Sweetheart' from Elvis Costello.

3. A BUNCH OF STIFF RECORDS
UK Stiff SEEZ 2.
Released 1977.
 Includes 'Less Than Zero' from Elvis Costello.

4. STIFFS LIVE STIFFS
UK Stiff GET 1.
Released February 1978.
 Includes 'I Just Don't Know What To Do With Myself' (Bacharach, David) and 'Miracle Man' (Costello) live from Elvis Costello, who also joins in on 'Sex And Drugs And Rock And Roll' (Dury) with Ian Dury.
 Reissued on Music For Pleasure MFP.50445 with different sleeve.

COMPILATIONS

5. HEROES AND COWARDS
ITALY Stiff SEEZ 0 (SEWL 1000).
Released 1978.
   Includes Less Than Zero/Mystery Dance/Alison from Elvis Costello.

8. BREAKING THE RULES
US Columbia A25-881.
Released 1980.
   Includes 'Big Tears' from Elvis Costello.
   Promotional compilation.

6. THAT SUMMER (Original Soundtrack)
UK Arista SPART 1088.
Released 1979.
   Includes (I Don't Want To Go To) Chelsea/Watching The Detectives from Elvis Costello.

7. AMERICATHON (Original soundtrack)
UK Lorimar CBS 70172.
US Lorimar JS 36174.
Released 1979.
   Includes (I Don't Want To Go To) Chelsea/Crawling To The U.S.A. from Elvis Costello.

9. HAPPY ROCK – O MAXIMO DA NEW WAVE
PORTUGAL Da Nova 10.014/5.
Released 1981.
   Includes 'Alison' from Elvis Costello.
   Double album on blue vinyl with t-shirt of sleeve design.

10. NME DANCIN' MASTER
UK NME NME 001.
Released 1981.
   Includes 'Big Sister' from Elvis Costello.
   Tape only compilation.

11. CONCERTS FOR THE PEOPLE OF KAMPUCHEA
UK Atlantic K60153.
US Atlantic 2-7005.
Released March 1981.
   Includes 'The Imposter' live from Elvis Costello.

15. PARTY PARTY (Original soundtrack)
UK A&M AMLH 68551.
Released December 1982.
   Includes 'Party Party' title track from Elvis Costello and The Attractions with The Royal Guard Horns.

12. FUNDAMENTAL FROLICS
UK BBC Records REB 435.
Released 1981.
   Includes 'Psycho Song' (Leon Payne) live at Apollo Theatre, London June 1, 1981, in aid of MENCAP/International Year Of The Disabled.

13. ROCK AGAINST RACISM'S GREATEST HITS
UK Virgin RAR – 1.
Released February 1982.
   Includes 'Goon Squad' from Elvis Costello.

14. NME MIGHTY REEL
UK NME NME 004.
Released November 1982.
   Includes 'Town Cryer' from Elvis Costello.
   Tape only compilation.

COMPILATIONS

PRODUCTION WORK

**1. MESSAGE TO YOU RUDY
(R. Thompson)/NITE KLUB
(J. Dammers, Specials)**
The Specials (Single).
UK Two-Tone CHS TT-5.
Released September 1979.
Produced by Elvis Costello.

2. THE SPECIALS
The Specials (LP).
UK Two-Tone CDL TT-5001.
US Chrysalis CHR 1265.
Released 1979.
Produced by Elvis Costello.

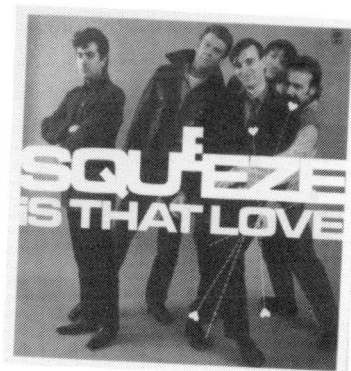

**3. IS THAT LOVE (Tilbrook/Difford)/
TRUST (Tilbrook/Difford)**
Squeeze (Single).
UK A&M AMS 8129.
Released 1981.
Produced by Roger Bechirian and Elvis Costello.

4. EAST SIDE STORY
Squeeze (LP).
UK A&M AMLH 64854.
US A&M SP-4854.
Released 1981.
Produced by Roger Bechirian and Elvis Costello.
    Backing vocals by Elvis Costello on 'Tempted' and 'There's No Tomorrow'.

**5. TEMPTED (Tilbrook/Difford)/
YAP.YAP.YAP. (Tilbrook/Difford)**
Squeeze (Single).
UK A&M AMS 8147.
Released 1981.
A-side produced by Roger Bechirian and Elvis Costello.
    Backing vocals on 'Tempted' by Elvis Costello.

PRODUCTION WORK

6. TEMPTED (Tilbrook/Difford)/ TRUST (Tilbrook/Difford)
Squeeze (Single).
US A&M AM-2345.
Released 1981.
Produced by Roger Bechirian and Elvis Costello.
   Backing vocals on 'Tempted' by Elvis Costello.

7. LABELLED WITH LOVE (Tilbrook/Difford)/SQUABS ON FORTY FAB (Tilbrook/Difford)
Squeeze (Single).
UK A&M AMS 8166.
Released 1981.
A-side produced by Roger Bechirian and Elvis Costello.

8. FOREVERMORE (R. Hodgens)/ AIM IN LIFE (K. McClusky)
The Bluebells (Single).
UK London LON 14.
Released October 1982.
B-side produced by Elvis Costello.
   See also listing No. 9 below.

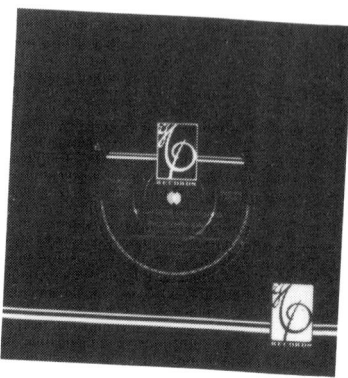

11. THE CAPTAIN AND THE KINGS (Brendan Behan)/FAITHFUL DEPARTED (P. Chevron)
Philip Chevron (LP).
UK IMP Records IMP 002.
Released December 1982.
Produced by Fairley/Imposter (Colin Fairley and Elvis Costello).
   B-side includes 'EC At The B.3'.

9. EVERYBODY'S SOMEBODY'S FOOL (R. Hodgens)
The Bluebells (Flexidisc).
UK London LONF 14 (LYN 12361).
Released October 1982.
Produced by Elvis Costello.
   Free flexidisc on transparent vinyl with initial quantities of 'Forevermore' single (see listing No. 8 above).

10. NME RACKET PACKET
(Cassette).
UK NME NME 006.
Released 1983.
Tape only compilation, includes The Bluebells' 'Aim In Life' (K. McClusky) produced by Elvis Costello.

12. SQUEEZE SINGLES
Squeeze (LP).
A&M Records AMLH 68552.
Released 1982.
   Includes 'Tempted', produced by Roger Bechirian and Elvis Costello.

**13. NELSON MANDELA (Dammers)/
BREAK DOWN THE DOOR!
(Dammers/Campbell/Bradbury)**
The Special A.K.A. (Single).
UK Two-Tone CHS TT-26.
Released March 1984.
Produced by Elvis Costello.
    Backing vocals by Elvis Costello.

PRODUCTION WORK

COVER VERSIONS

1. ALISON (Costello)/MOMMA (Christian, Walton)
Barry Christian (Single).
UK Mercury 6007 161.
Released 1977.

2. GIRLS TALK (Costello)/BAD IS BAD (Lewis)
Dave Edmunds (Single).
UK Swansong SSK 19418.
Released 1979.

COVER VERSIONS

3. JUST A MEMORY (Costello)/WHO CARES (The Shakin' Pyramids)
The Shakin' Pyramids (Single).
UK Virgin VS 505.
Released 1982.

5. SHIPBUILDING (C. Langer, Costello)/MEMORIES OF YOU (Blake, Razal)
Robert Wyatt (Single).
UK Rough Trade RT 115.
Released September 1982.

4. WASHING THE DEFECTIVES
The Beatles, Costello (EP).
US Pious JP 310.
Released 1978.
  Does not actually include any Costello material, despite the title. 'Thanks to Declan' on the sleeve.

6. SHATTERPROOF (Costello)/LOOK AT THAT CAR (Bremner, Birch)
Billy Bremner (Single).
UK Arista ARIST 557.
Released March 1984.

7. DUSTY SPRINGFIELD
(LP).
Possibly no release yet, includes 'Losing You' (Costello).

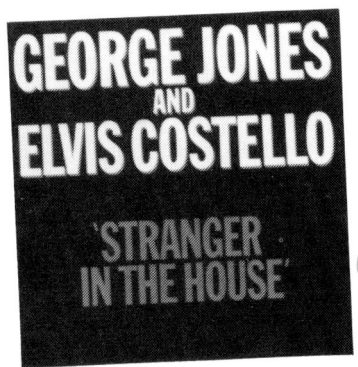

11. MAD LOVE
Linda Ronstadt (LP).
UK Asylum K52210.
Released 1980.
    Includes Party Girl/Talking In The Dark (both Costello).

12. FAR FROM THE HURTING KIND
Tracie (LP).
UK Respond.
Released May 1984.
    Includes '(I Love You) When You Sleep' (Costello).

8. STRANGER IN THE HOUSE (Costello)/A DRUNK CAN'T BE A MAN (G. Jones)
George Jones (Single).
UK Epic S-EPC 8560.
Released April 1980.
Re-released in picture sleeve March 1982.

9. MY VERY SPECIAL GUESTS
George Jones (LP).
UK Epic EPC 83163.
US Epic 35544.
Released 1979.
    Includes 'Stranger In The House' (Costello).

10. LIVING IN THE U.S.A.
Linda Ronstadt (LP).
UK Asylum K53085.
US Asylum.
Released September 1978.
    Includes 'Alison' (Costello).

COVER VERSIONS

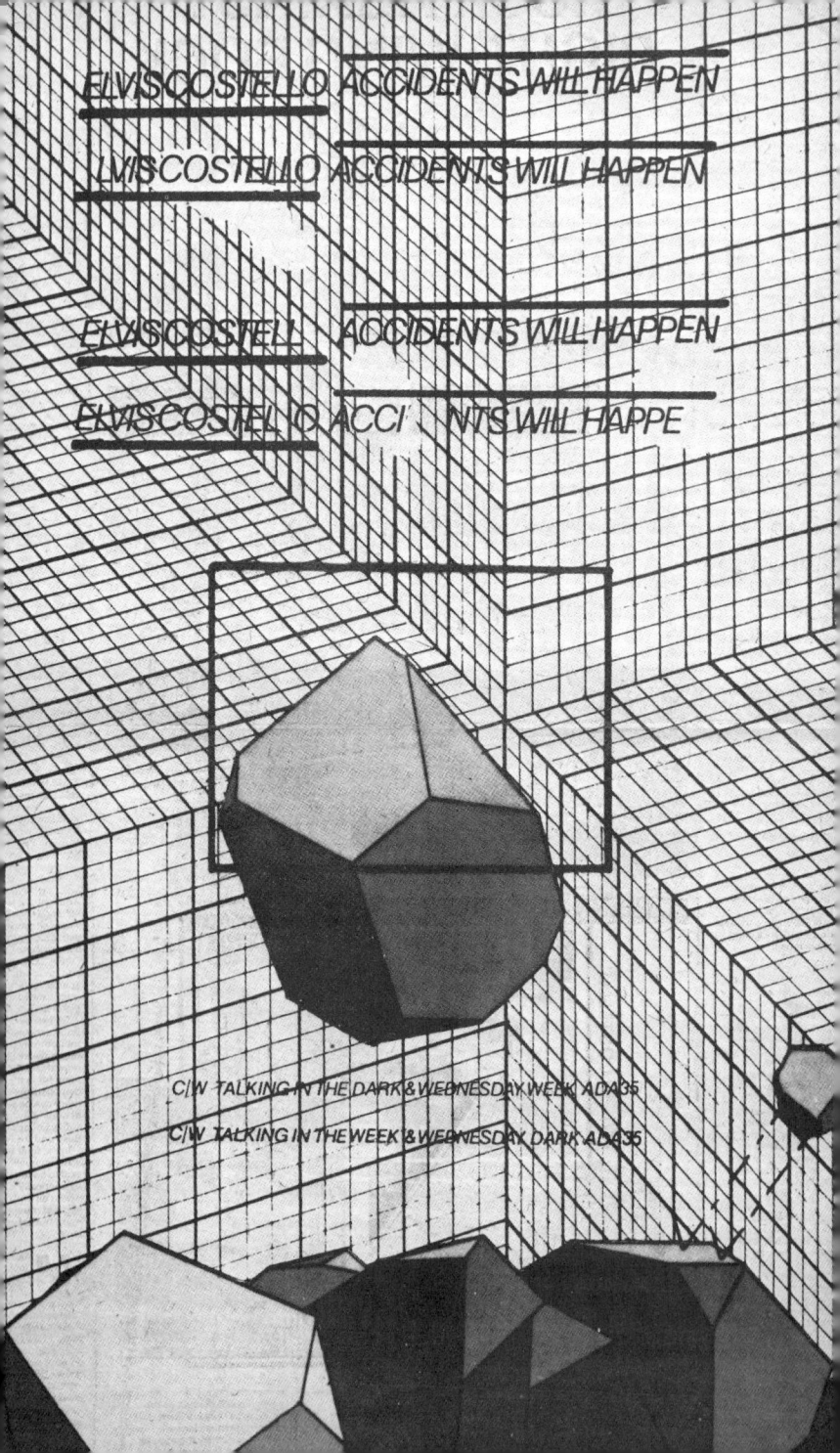

COLLABORATIONS

1. THIS IS YOUR LIFE
The Twist (LP).
UK Polydor 2383 552.
Released 1979.
 Includes Elvis Costello on vocals.

2. MY VERY SPECIAL GUESTS
George Jones (LP).
UK Epic EPC 83163.
US Epic 35544.
Released 1979.
 Includes George Jones and Elvis Costello duet on 'Stranger In The House' (Costello).

3. STRANGER IN THE HOUSE (Costello)/A DRUNK CAN'T BE A MAN (G. Jones)
George Jones (Single).
UK Epic S-EPC 8560.
Released April 1980.
 Duet with Elvis Costello on A-side. Re-released in picture sleeve March 1982.

4. EAST SIDE STORY
Squeeze (LP).
UK A&M AMLH 64854.
US A&M SP-4854.
Released 1981.
 Backing vocals by Elvis Costello on 'Tempted' and 'There's No Tomorrow.

5. TEMPTED (Tilbrook, Difford)/YAP.YAP.YAP. (Tilbrook, Difford)
Squeeze (Single).
UK A&M AMS 8147.
Released 1981.
 Backing vocals on 'Tempted' by Elvis Costello.

6. TEMPTED (Tilbrook, Difford)/TRUST (Tilbrook, Difford)
Squeeze (Single).
US A&M AM-2345.
Released 1981.
 Backing vocals on 'Tempted' by Elvis Costello.

7. BLACK COFFEE IN BED (Tilbrook, Difford)/THE HUNT (Tilbrook, Difford)
Squeeze (Single).
UK A&M AMS 8219.
Released 1982.
 Backing vocals on A-side by Elvis Costello.

8. TOMORROW'S (JUST ANOTHER DAY) (Smyth, Barson) Warp mix/BLUE BEAST (Thompson) Warp mix/TOMORROW'S (JUST ANOTHER DAY) (Smyth, Barson)/MADNESS (IS ALL IN THE MIND) (Foreman)
Madness (Single).
UK Stiff BUY IT 169.
Released February 1983.
 Second 'Tomorrow's (Just Another Day)' is a reworked version with Elvis Costello on guest vocals.

ELVIS COSTELLO. MASTERPIECE?

"IMPERIAL BEDROOM." ON COLUMBIA RECORDS AND TAPES.
ELVIS COSTELLO IS ON TOUR. JUDGE FOR YOURSELF.

Produced by Geoff Emerick. From an original idea by Elvis Costello. "Columbia" is a trademark of CBS Inc. © 1982 CBS Inc.

BOOTLEGS

1. ACCIDENTS • APRIL 1978 (Double)
Impossible Recordworks 2-28.
Recorded at London Roundhouse, excellent mono, de luxe b&w cover.
   Side One: 1. Stranger In The House/2. Oliver's Army/3. Accidents Will Happen/4. Waiting For The End Of The World/5. No Action.
   Side Two: 6. This Year's Girl/7. Lip Service/8. Less Than Zero/9. Big Tears/10. Hand In Hand.
   Side Three: 11. The Beat/12. Red Shoes/13. Alison/14. Miracle Man/15. Chelsea.
   Side Four: 16. Mystery Dance/17. Watching The Detectives/18. You Belong To Me/19. Pump It Up.

2. ARMED AND DANGEROUS • LIVE 1977
Impossible Recordworks 1-32
Excellent stereo, de luxe b&w cover.
   Side One: 1. Welcome To The Working Week/2. Red Shoes/3. Waiting For The End Of The World/4. No Action/5. The Beat/6. Less Than Zero/7. Radio Radio/8. You Belong To Me.
   Side Two: 9. Lipstick Vogue/10. Watching The Detectives/11. Pump It Up/12. Miracle Man/13. Mystery Dance/14. No Dancing.

3. BIG OPPORTUNITY
79-116/117M.
Good mono, pressed on multi-coloured vinyl.
   Side One: 1. Big Opportunity/2. Moods For Moderns/3. Green Shirt/4. Party Girl/5. Girlschool/6. Accidents Will Happen.
   Side Two: 7. Big Boys/8. Goon Squad/9. Oliver's Army/10. Peace, Love And Understanding/11. Radio Radio.

4. BIG SISTER
Punktured PU6001.
Excellent stereo, one-sided 33 with b&w picture sleeve – same as later commercial studio release.
   Side One: 1. Big Sister (2'17").

5. BLITZKRIEG • FRANCE 1979. (Triple set).
Thunderbolt Productions SXN 9321.
Paris June 1979, Cannes and Montpellier December 1979.
Very good mono and stereo, box set, blue vinyl, de luxe b&w sleeve. 500 copies, 250 numbered.
   Side One: 1. I Stand Accused/2. Hand In Hand/3. Opportunity.
   Side Two: 4. Green Shirt/5. I Don't Want To Go To Chelsea/6. B Movie.
   Side Three: 7. So Young/8. Oliver's Army/9. Stand Up For.
   Side Four: 10. Girl's Talk/11. Five Gears/12. Clown Time Is Over.
   Side Five: 13. Watching The Detectives/14. Possession.
   Side Six: 15. Love For Tender/16. Gangster/17. I Need The Human Touch.

6. CORNERED ON PLASTIC
Red Shoes Records SELL1.
Excellent mono EP, pressed on red vinyl, b&w picture sleeve.
   Side One: 1. Wave A White Flag/2. Lip Service (acoustic solo demos for Radio London, Spring 1977).
   Side Two: 3. Hoover Factory (electric solo session for Capital Radio, London, Autumn 1977)/4. Really Mystified (BBC session, Autumn 1978).

7. DELUXE
GHL 25/L2716.
Varies between good mono to very good stereo.
De luxe colour cover, 'Girls Talk' and 'Opportunity' are listed twice on the sleeve.
   Side One: 1. Love Me Tender/2. Human Touch/3. The Imposter/4. Secondary Modern/5. Girls Talk/6. King Horse/7. Temptation/8. Opportunity/9. Five Gears In Reverse.
   Side Two: 10. I Can't Stand Up/11. Clowntime Over/12. Possession/13. B Movie/14. I Stand Accused/15. Motel Matches/16. High Fidelity.

8. EXIT (Double)
Toasted 2S919.
De luxe colour front sleeve.
   Sides One & Two: 'The Kornyfone Radio Hour' (TAKRL 901), a re-release.
   Sides Three & Four: 'Armed And Dangerous' (Impossible Recordworks 1-32), a re-release.

9. ELVIS AND FRIENDS VISIT WASHINGTON
Phoenix 44779.
A copy of 'Elvis Goes To Washington And Dave Edmunds And Rockpile Don't' (Pacifist 7978) with a de luxe full colour cover, excellent stereo.

10. ELVIS COSTELLO
Cowboy Discs NICK 1.
Excellent recording, but crackles. b & w picture sleeve.
Side One: 1. Stranger In The House (studio, stereo).
Side Two: 2. I Just Don't Know What To Do With Myself (studio, mono)/ 3. Honky Tonkin'; Honky Tonk Blues (mono, live).

11. ELVIS COSTELLO
TAKRL 928.
Recorded at Hot Club, Philadelphia, good stereo, de luxe b&w sleeve.
Side One: 1. Welcome To The Working Week/2. Red Shoes/3. Waiting For The End Of The World/4. No Action/ 5. Less Than Zero/6. The Beast (sic).
Side Two: 7. Roadette Song/8. Blame It On Cain/9. Little Triggers/10. Radio Radio.

12. ELVIS COSTELLO
Toasted 2S903.
Re-release of 'Accidents' (IMP 2-28) with a de luxe colour cover.

13. ELVIS GOES TO WASHINGTON AND DAVE EDMUNDS AND ROCKPILE DON'T (Double)
Pacifist 7978.
Sides One-Three Costello at the Warren Theater, Washington D.C., 1978 (not 1979 as listed on sleeve). Side Four Rockpile in New York, March 1978. Excellent stereo.
Side One: 1. Pump It Up/2. Waiting For The End Of The World/3. No Action/ 4. Less Than Zero/5. The Beat/6. Red Shoes.
Side Two: 7. I Don't Want To Go To Chelsea/8. Hand In Hand/9. Little Triggers/10. Radio Radio/11. You Belong to Me/12. Lipstick Vogue.
Side Three: 13. Watching The Detectives/14. Mystery Dance/15. Miracle Man/16. Blame It On Cain/17. Chemistry Class.
Side Four: 18. Down, Down, Down/ 19. I Knew The Bride/20. Deborah/21. Breaking Glass (with Nick Lowe)/22. Let It Rock (with Keith Richard)/23. Heart Of The City.

14. 50,000,000 ELVIS FANS CAN'T BE WRONG (Double)
EL 5000.
Sides One and Two from Capital Radio, London, Granada TV, Eric's Club Liverpool, Top Of The Pops, 4 Ackers Club, Marcey, New York, 1977. Sides Three and Four from the Agora Club, Cleveland, Ohio, December 5, 1977. Excellent stereo, a few tracks excellent mono.
Side One: 1. Hoover Factory/2. You Belong To Me/3. Radio Radio/ 4. Mystery Dance/5. Red Shoes/6. Less Than Zero/7. Blame It On Cain/8. Alison/ 9. I Don't Want To Go To Chelsea/ 10. Watching The Detectives/11. Lip Service.
Side Two: 12. Watching The Detectives/13. Tiny Steps/14. Big Tears/ 15. Roadette Song/16. Living In Paradise/ 17. Little Triggers/18. Medley: Welcome To The Working Week/Red Shoes/Hand In Hand.
Side Three: 19. Waiting For The End Of The World/20. No Action/21. Less Than Zero/22. The Beat/23. No Dancing/ 24. Big Tears/25. Little Triggers/ 26. Radio Radio.
Side Four: 27. You Belong To Me/ 28. Pump It Up/29. Lipstick Vogue/ 30. Watching The Detectives/31. Miracle Man/32. Mystery Dance.

15. 50,000 ELVIS FANS CAN'T BE WRONG (Double)
SX TT 979.
Same as listing No. 14 above, with b&w de luxe cover. Faded back sleeve and blurred lettering suggest this is a bootleg of a bootleg!

16. HATE YOU LIVE
EC 9000.
Side One excellent mono, Side Two excellent stereo. De luxe b&w sleeve.

Side One: 1. Goon Squad/2. Big Opportunity/3. Oliver's Army/4. Busy Body/5. Two Little Hitlers/6. Green Shirt/ 7. Big Boys/8. Party Girl.
Side Two: 9. Wednesday Week/10. Talking In The Dark/11. Stranger In The House/12. Neat Neat Neat/13. Radio Sweetheart/14. Night Rally/15. Funny Valentine.
Side One live, Side Two studio tracks released elsewhere but not available in the US at the time.

17. HIDING UNDER COVERS
Mr. Normal Brain Records BRAIN-1.
Side One excellent stereo, Side Two excellent mono, b&w picture sleeve.
Side One: 1. Price Of Love/2. Slow Down.
Side Two: 3. I Got You/4. I'll Fly Away.

18. HONKY TONK DEMOS
Compact DRP 3974.
Excellent stereo, taken from Charlie Gillett's 'Honky Tonk' show on Radio London.
Side One: 1. Lip Service/2. Jump Up/ 3. Mystery Dance.
Side Two: 4. Wave A White Flag/ 5. Blame It On Cain/6. Poison Moon.

19. THE KORNYFONE RADIO HOUR
TAKRL 901.
FM broadcast from the El Mocambo, Toronto, excellent stereo, de luxe b&w cover.
Side One: 1. Mystery Dance/ 2. Waiting For The End Of The World/ 3. Welcome To The Working Week/ 4. Less Than Zero/5. The Beat/6. Lip Service/7. I Don't Want To Go To Chelsea.
Side Two: 8. Little Triggers/9. Radio Radio/10. Vogue/11. Watchin' The Detectives/12. Heart Of The City/ 13. Miracle Man.
'The Beat' and 'I Don't Want To Go To Chelsea' not listed on the sleeve.

20. THE LAST FOXTROT
Rubber Robot RR002.
Live with Nick Lowe in San Francisco, June 7, 1978. Excellent stereo.
Side One: 1. Goon Squad/2. Less Than Zero/3. Chelsea/4. Pump It Up/ 5. Radio Radio/6. Lipstick Vogue/ 7. Watching the Detectives.
Side Two: 8. Party Girl/9. I'm Not Angry/ 10. So It Goes/11. Fool Too Long/ 12. Breaking Glass/13. Heart Of The City.

21. LAST YEAR'S MODEL
Time Warp 1.
From El Mocambo, Toronto, 1978 FM broadcast.
Originally plain sleeve, later with picture sleeve, 500 copies, excellent mono.

Side One: 1. Mystery Dance/ 2. Waiting For The End Of The World.
Side Two: 3. Welcome To The Working Week/4. Radio Radio.

22. LIKE BUDDY HOLLY ON ACID
Rubber Robot RR 002.
A re-release of 'The Last Foxtrot'.

23. LIVE AT THE PALOMINO (Double)
Centrifugal 12CENT-03.
From Palomino Club, Hollywood, February 1979.
Excellent mono, de luxe colour sleeve.
Side One: 1. Big Boys/2. Hand In Hand/3. Opportunity/4. Accidents Will Happen/5. Goon Squad.
Side Two: 6. Two Little Hitlers/7. The Beat/8. Green Shirt/9. I Stand Accused/10. Radio Radio.
Side Three: 11. Stranger In The House/12. Psycho/13. If I Could Put Them All Together/14. Motel Matches.
Side Four: 15. He'll Have To Go/ 16. Girls Talk/17. Alison/18. I Don't Want To Go To Chelsea/19. Mystery Dance.

24. OUR AIM IS TRUE
Stiff (!) Records S3230.
Studio out-takes, excellent stereo, made up to look like an official promo, de luxe b&w sleeve.
Side One: 1. Third Rate Romance/ 2. Living In Paradise/3. Radio Soul/ 4. Radio Soul (Take 2)/5. Pay It Back/ 6. Imagination Is A Powerful Deceiver/ 7. Imagination Is A Powerful Deceiver (Take 2).
Side Two: 8. Imagination Is A Powerful Deceiver (Take 3)/9. Third Rate Romance (Take 2)/10. Knockin' On Heaven's Door/ 11. I'm Packing Up/12. I'm Packing Up (Take 2)/13. Don't Stop The Band/ 14. Just Don't Know What To Do With Myself.

25. RADIO BLAST EP
Bang 4.
Studio out-takes from 'Get Happy!!' album. Colour photo-copied picture sleeve, excellent stereo.
Side One: 1. B Movie/2. Possession.
Side Two: 3. High Fidelity/4. Beaten To The Punch.

26. RADIO RADIO
EC 2240.
Excellent stereo.
Side One: 1. Mystery Dance/ 2. Waiting For The End Of The World/ 3. Welcome To The Working Week/ 4. Less Than Zero/5. The Beat/6. Lip Service.
Side Two: 7. Little Triggers/8. Radio Radio/9. Lipstick Vogue/10. Watching The Detectives/11. Pump It Up/12. Heart

BOOTLEGS

Of The City/13. Miracle Man.
  Sleeve also lists 'I Don't Want To Go To Chelsea', but it is not included on the album.

27. SATURATED
Excitable Recordworks 4518-1.
Re-release of 'The Kornyfone Radio Show' (TAKRL 901), de luxe b&w cover, excellent stereo.

28. SHAKEN, NOT STIRRED
Unfit Artists.
Live from Swedish TV, September 30, 1977, Hope And Anchor, London, May 14, 1980, and Palomino, Hollywood, February 16, 1979.
Excellent mono, de luxe b&w sleeve.
  Side One: 1. Watching The Detectives/2. Interview/3. Mystery Dance/4. Little Sister/5. Don't Look Back.
  Side Two: 6. Stranger In The House/7. Psycho/8. Put Them All Together/9. Motel Matches/10. He'll Have To Go/11. Girls Talk.

29. SOMETHING NEW
EC-LIE-003.
From King Biscuit Flower Hour radio broadcast, 1980. Excellent mono.
  Side One: 1. Temptation/2. Help Me/3. I Stand Accused/4. One Fine Heartache/5. Secondary Modern/6. High Fidelity/7. Lipstick Vogue/8. Waiting For The End Of The World.
  Side Two: 9. Walk And Don't Look Back/10. Girls Talk/11. Watching The Detectives/12. You Belong To Me/13. Oliver's Army/14. Pump It Up.
  Title 'You Lied To Me' listed on the sleeve but not included on the album.

30. SOMETHING NEW
EC-LIE-003.
Re-release as a b&w picture disc using the original pressing's paper insert front and back. A second b&w picture disc re-release uses the original pressing's paper insert minus the song titles on Side One and b&w Elvis photo on Side Two.

31. A SUPER EP
Super Records 101.
From studio out-takes. Red vinyl and b&w picture sleeve, excellent stereo.
  Side One: 1. (I Don't Want To Go To) Chelsea/2. You Belong To Me (Live).
  Side Two: 3. Living In Paradise/4, Hoover Factory.

32. WE'RE ALL CREEPS
78-163/164M.
Live, pressed on clear vinyl with no labels, excellent mono although cover says stereo.
  Side One: 1. Mystery Dance/2. Waiting For The End Of The World/3. Nite Rider/4. No Action/5. Less Than Zero.
  Side Two: 6. The Best/7. I Don't Wanna Go To Chelsea/8. This Year's Girl/9. Little Triggers.

Elvis Costello and the Attractions

New Single

I Wanna Be Loved

Includes Turning The Town Red

Theme Music From Granada T.V. Series "Scully"

F-Beat

7"- XX35 / 12"- XX35T

TAPES

Release dates and contents are as for the corresponding albums.

1. MY AIM IS TRUE
Stiff ZSEEZ 3.
Columbia ALT 35037.

2. THIS YEAR'S MODEL
Radar RADC 3.
F-Beat XXC 4.
Columbia JCT 35331.
Columbia PCT 35331.

3. ARMED FORCES
Radar RADC 14.
F-Beat XXC 5.
Columbia JCT 35331.
Columbia PCT 35331.

4. GET HAPPY!!
F-Beat XXC 1.
Columbia JCT 36347.
Columbia PCT 36347.
IMP FIEND CASS 24.

5. TAKING LIBERTIES
Columbia JCT 36839.

6. TEN BLOODY MARYS AND TEN HOW'S YOUR FATHERS
F-Beat XXC 6.
IMP FIEND CASS 27.

7. TRUST
F-Beat XXC 11.
Columbia JCT 37051.

8. ALMOST BLUE
F-Beat XXC 13.
Columbia JCT 37051.
IMP FIEND CASS 33.

9. IMPERIAL BEDROOM
F-Beat XXC 17.
Columbia JCT 38157.

10. PUNCH THE CLOCK
F-Beat XXC 19.
Columbia FCT 38897.

11. GOODBYE CRUEL WORLD
UK F-Beat ZK70317.

ELVIS COSTELLO
OUT NOW

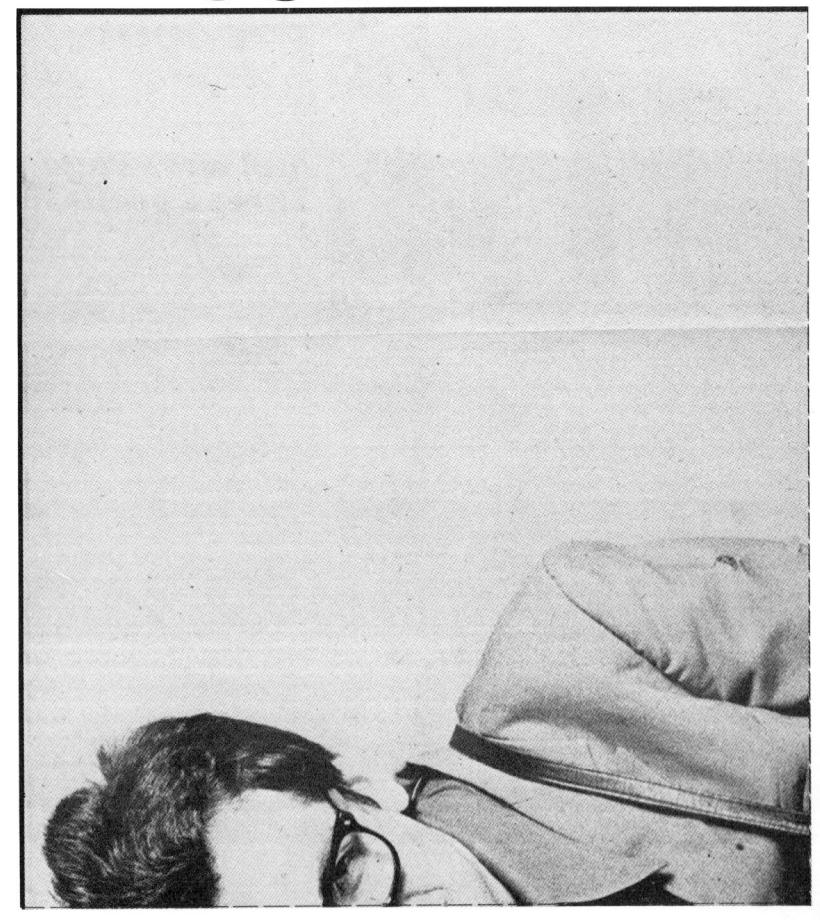

FILMS

1. AMERICATHON
Starring Harvey Korman, Fred Willard, Peter Riegert, Zane Buzby, Nancy Morgan, John Ritter.
Special guest appearance by Elvis Costello.
Directed by Neil Israel.
Producer Joe Roth, executive producer Ed Rosen.
A Lorimar Production.
With songs by Eddie Money, The Beach Boys, Elvis Costello and Nick Lowe.

2. SCULLY
Granada Television Series (1984).
Written by Alan Bleasdale.
Starring Andrew Schofield with guest appearances by Kenny Dalgleish and Elvis Costello.
Produced by Steve Morrison.
Directed by Les Chatfield.
Includes 'Turning The Town Red' (Costello) performed by Elvis Costello and The Attractions as theme music.

MY AIM IS TRUE

To collect your free dramatic action pix of Elvis,
cut out this ad and stick it on your bedroom wall as
shown in the diagram. For sheets 5,6,4,3 see this week's
_____ and _____

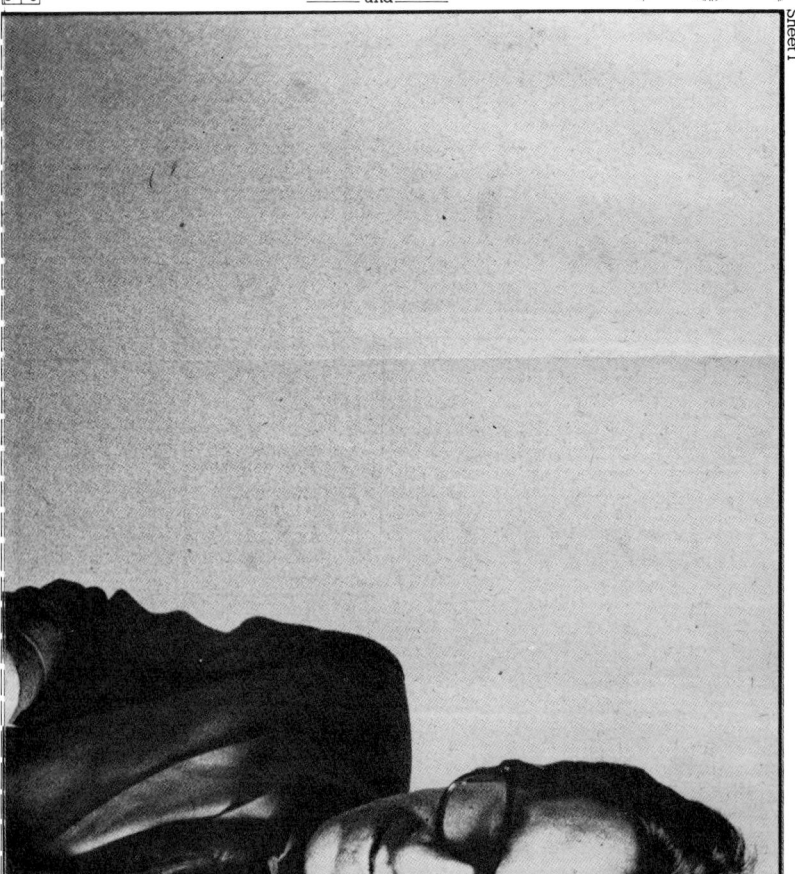

Sheet 1

BIBLIOGRAPHY

1. ELVIS COSTELLO – A SINGING DICTIONARY
Music Book.
Plangent Visions 1980.
Music and lyrics to all the songs from 'My Aim Is True', 'This Year's Model', 'Armed Forces', 'Get Happy!!' and 'Taking Liberties', plus an unrecorded song 'That's What Friends Are For'.

2. ELVIS COSTELLO – EVERYDAY I WRITE THE SONGS
Music Book.
Plangent Visions 1983.
Music and lyrics to all the songs from 'Trust', 'Imperial Bedroom' and 'Punch The Clock'.

3. ELVIS COSTELLO – A COMPLETELY FALSE BIOGRAPHY BASED ON RUMOUR, INNUENDO AND LIES
By Krista Reese.
Proteus Publishing Ltd 1981.
ISBN 0.906071 62 3.
Believe the title.

INDEX
TO SOME TITLES

As there is so much variation in the album track listings and singles releases from country to country, this index shows exactly what tracks can be found where. All official releases are included, not only Costello compositions, and the reference numbers correspond to the particular listing in each section. The letter prefix relates the reference number to the section, 'A' for Singles, 'B' for Albums, 'C' for Compilations, and 'D' for Cover Versions.

ACCIDENTS WILL HAPPEN A24, A25, A26, A27, A42, A48, B1, B2, B7, B17, C1, C5, C9, D1.
ALISON A24, A25, A26, A27, A48, B7, B8, B17.
ALMOST BLUE B18, B19.
... AND IN EVERY HOME B18, B19.

BEATEN TO THE PUNCH B9, B10.
BEYOND BELIEF A61, B18, B19.
BIG BOYS B7, B8.
BIG SISTER A55, C13.
BIG SISTER'S CLOTHES B14.
BIG TEARS A15, A17, B11, B13, B21, C8.
BLACK AND WHITE WORLD B9, B10, B11, B13, B21.
BLAME IT ON CAIN A8, A9, A10, B1, B2.
BLUES KEEP CALLING A54.
B MOVIE B9, B10.
BOY WITH A PROBLEM B18, B19.
BROWN TO BLUE B15, B16.
BUSY BODIES B7, B8.

CHARM SCHOOL B20.
CHEMISTRY CLASS B7, B8.
CLEAN MONEY A40, A43, B11, B12, B13, B21.
CLOWNTIME IS OVER A33, B9, B10, B11, B13, B21.
CLUBLAND A40, A43, B14.
COLOUR OF THE BLUES A50, B15, B16.
CRAWLING TO THE U.S.A. B11, B13, B21, C7.
CRY, CRY, CRY A53.

DIFFERENT FINGER B14.
DR. LUTHER'S ASSISTANT A34, A35, A37, B11, B13, B21.

EVERYDAY I WRITE THE BOOK A67, A68, A69, A70, B20.

FISH 'N' CHIP PAPER B14.
FIVE GEARS IN REVERSE B9, B10.
FROM A WHISPER TO A SCREAM A41, A46, A47, B14.
FROM HEAD TO TOE A63.

GETTING MIGHTY CROWDED A32, A33, A36, A39, B11, B12, B13, B21.
GHOST TRAIN A35, A37, B11, B13, B21.
GIRLS TALK A28, A29, A30, A31, B11, B13, B21, D2.
GOOD YEAR FOR THE ROSES A49, A50, A51, B15, B16.
GOON SQUAD B7, B8, C10.
GREEN SHIRT B7, B8, B17.

HAND IN HAND B3, B4, B5.
HEATHEN TOWN A67, A68, A69, A70.
HIGH FIDELITY A32, A33, A36, B9, B10.
HONEY HUSH B15, B16.
HONKY TONK GIRL A54.
HOOVER FACTORY A40, A43, B11,

INDEX TO SOME TITLES

B13, B21.
HOW MUCH I LIED B15, B16.
HUMAN HANDS B18, B19.
HUMAN TOUCH B9, B10.

I CAN'T STAND UP FOR FALLING DOWN A28, A29, A30, A31, B17.
(I DON'T WANT TO GO TO) CHELSEA A12, A13, B3, B4, B5, B6, B11, C6, C7.
I JUST DON'T KNOW WHAT TO DO WITH MYSELF C4.
I'M NOT ANGRY B1, B2.
IMPERIAL BEDROOM A57, A64.
I'M YOUR TOY A53, A54, B15, B16, B17.
I STAND ACCUSED B9, B10.

JUST A MEMORY A35, A37, B11, B13, B21, D3.

KID ABOUT IT B18, B19.
KING HORSE A30, B9, B10.
KING OF THIEVES B20.

LESS THAN ZERO A1, A42, B1, B2, B6, C3, C5.
LET THEM ALL TALK A71, A72, A73, A74, A75, B20.
LIP SERVICE B3, B4, B5, B6.
LIPSTICK VOGUE B3, B4, B5, B6.
LITTLE SAVAGE B18, B19.
LITTLE TRIGGERS B3, B4, B5, B6.
LIVING IN PARADISE B3, B4, B5.
LOVE FOR TENDER B9, B10.
LOVER'S WALK B14.
LOVE WENT MAD B20.
LUXEMBOURG A44, A46, A47, B14.

MAN CALLED UNCLE B9, B10.
MAN OUT OF TIME A56, A57, A58, A59, A60, A61, A62, B18, B19.
MIRACLE MAN A7, B1, B2, B6, C4.
MOODS FOR MODERNS B7, B8.
MOTEL MATCHES B9, B10.
MOUTH ALMIGHTY B20.
MY FUNNY VALENTINE A21, A22, A23, B11, B13, B21.
MY SHOES KEEP WALKING BACK TO YOU A54.
MYSTERY DANCE A3, A4, A5, A8, A9, A10, B1, B2, B6, C5.

NEAT, NEAT, NEAT A14.
NEW AMSTERDAM A34, A35, A37, A38, B9, B10.
NEW LACE SLEEVES A41, B14.
NIGHT RALLY A13, B3, B4, B11.
NIGHT TIME A68, A70.
NO ACTION B3, B4, B5.
NO DANCING B1, B2.

OLIVER'S ARMY A21, A22, B7, B8.
OPPORTUNITY B9, B10.

PARTY GIRL B7, B8.
PARTY PARTY A64, A65, C15.
PAY IT BACK A5, B1, B2.

PEACE IN OUR TIME A76.
PIDGIN ENGLISH B18, B19.
PILLS AND SOAP A66, B20.
POSSESSION B9, B10.
PRETTY WORDS A41, B14.
PSYCHO A52, C12.
PUMP IT UP A15, B3, B4, B5, B6, B17.

RADIO RADIO A16, A18, B5, B6, B13, B21.
RADIO SWEETHEART A1, A39, B11, B12, B13, B21, C2.
RIOT ACT B9, B10.

SECONDARY MODERN A30, B9, B10.
SENIOR SERVICE B7, B8.
SHABBY DOLL B18, B19.
SHIPBUILDING A74, B20, C5.
SHOT WITH HIS OWN GUN B14.
SITTIN' AND THINKIN' B15, B16.
SNEAKY FEELINGS B1, B2.
STRANGER IN THE HOUSE A14, B11, B13, B21, D8, D9.
STRICT TIME B14.
SUCCESS B15, B16.
SUNDAY'S BEST A25, B7, B8, B11.
SWEET DREAMS A50, A52, B15, B16.

TALKING IN THE DARK A20, A24, A26, B11, B12, B13, B21.
TEARS BEFORE BEDTIME B18, B19.
TEMPTATION B9, B10.
(THE ANGELS WANNA WEAR MY) RED SHOES A3, A4, A42, B1, B2, C1.
THE BEAT B3, B4, B5, B6.
THE ELEMENT WITHIN HER B20.
THE FLIRTING KIND A71, A72, A75.
THE GREATEST THING B20.
THE IMPOSTER B9, B10, C11.
THE INVISIBLE MAN B20.
THE LONG HONEYMOON B18, B19.
THE LOVED ONES B18, B19.
THE STAMPING GROUND A55.
THE WORLD AND HIS WIFE B20.
THE WORLD OF BROKEN HEARTS A63.
THIS YEAR'S GIRL A17, B3, B4, B5.
TINY STEPS A13, A18, B11, B13, B21.
T.K.O. (BOXING DAY) B20.
TONIGHT THE BOTTLE LET ME DOWN B15, B16.
TOO FAR GONE B15, B16.
TWO LITTLE HITLERS B7, B8.
TOWN CRYER A56, A57, A62, B18, B19, C14.

WAITING FOR THE END OF THE WORLD B1, B2, B6.
WATCHING THE DETECTIVES A8, A9, A10, A11, A27, A42, B2, B4, B6, B7, B13, B21, C1, C6.
WATCH YOUR STEP A44, A45, B14.
WEDNESDAY WEEK A20, A24, A26, A38, B11, B13, B21.
WELCOME TO THE WORKING WEEK A2, B1, B2, B6.
(WHAT'S SO FUNNY 'BOUT) PEACE,

LOVE AND UNDERSTANDING A19, A23, B8, B13, B17, B21.
WHITE KNUCKLES B14.
WHY DON'T YOU LOVE ME (LIKE YOU USED TO DO) A50, B15, B16.
WITHERED AND DIED A76.
WONDERING A53.

YOU BELONG TO ME A12, B3, B4, B5, B6.
YOU LITTLE FOOL A55, B18, B19.
YOU'LL NEVER BE A MAN A41, B14.
YOUR ANGEL STEPS OUT OF HEAVEN A49.

INDEX TO SOME TITLES